Cosmic Community

Celebrating Kindness

By Karen Molenaar Terrell

This was The first printing + there were still some rough patches.

Thank you for being our neighbor!

Karen

(The Bow Community is on pp 40-41.)

Dedicated to the community of family and friends who keep me inspired, nurture the good in me, and share their kindness with the world.

There Are Moments of Such Beauty

There are moments of such beauty
I'm moved to tears.
Little bursts of light in the darkness
that are bigger than my fears.
To be alive to see even a moment
of the beauty that can be
is worth the other moments
of darkness in between.

December 6, 2023

This morning I felt impelled to get out of the house and go for a drive. I ended up at the mall in Bellingham with the vague idea that I might go Christmas shopping.

As I headed into Macy's a young woman approached me – she looked scared. She said her baby was locked in the car with her keys and she asked me if I could let security know. I went into Macy's and let the customer service people know the situation. They needed to know the model of the car and where it was parked, so I went back out and asked the young mother if I could watch her car and baby while she went inside to talk to the customer service people. She thanked me and I took up my post by her car.

When I looked in the window I saw her baby was crying – so I said, "Hi Sweetie! I'm right here with you!" and she started giggling then and smiling at me. There was a little toy suction cupped to the window and the baby reached up and started playing with the toy – like she was playing with me – and we spent the next minute or so laughing at her toy together.

The baby's mom came out then, and pretty soon folks in uniforms joined her at her car to help her.

And the thought occurred to me that maybe that was the whole reason I'd felt like I'd needed to drive and ended up at the mall – I hardly ever go there, and it was weird for me to decide to go there today.

I bought a red vest and a new pair of jeans and then started my drive home.

And the clouds and the rain and the gray evening light enveloped me in a peaceful bubble. I'd put in a CD of hymns sung by a pair of young brothers with a youthful energy, and as I listened to the hymns I thought of my mom and remembered all the times she'd sung those hymns to me. I could feel her love with me.

As I drove through the Chuckanut Hills, I thought of the hikes I'd taken with Dad and felt his love, too. And then I remembered driving this same route when I was bringing the sons home from swimming lessons when they were preschoolers, and I could almost hear them laughing with each other in the back seat. It seemed a lifetime ago, and just like yesterday.

The young men on the CD sang, "He leadeth me, O blessed thought! O words with heav'nly comfort fraught..." (words by Joseph H. Gilmore). And suddenly I felt myself connected to all the other people in the cars moving with me on I-5. And for a moment our kinship with each other was so clear to me. I felt us all moving together in a cosmic murmuration. Normally I try to exit onto the backroads, but I found myself passing the exit I might normally have taken and I realized I WANTED to be with the other folks on I-5.

My drive home was other-worldly and beautiful.

December 18, 2023

One of the first places I ever visited in Bellingham was Tony's Coffee Shop in the Fairhaven district. I'm guessing this was in 1983. A year or so before we were married, I surprised my then-boyfriend Scott, who had graduated from Western Washington University, with a drive to Bellingham. It was a really fun day for us. Scott gave me a tour of the WWU campus, and then took me into Fairhaven and showed me his favorite haunts. Tony's was one of them.

We didn't know then that someday we would move "up north" and live 20 minutes from Fairhaven.

Fairhaven is one of my favorite places now. I never fail to find happy pups, kind people, and joy there. And Tony's has been one of my most favorite places of all.

Over the weekend Tony's (more lately known as The Old Independent Coffeehouse) and the Harris Cafe next door caught fire. There's nothing left now but the brick shell of the building the coffee shop and cafe were housed in. I'm still trying to wrap my head around it.

I thought I'd share some stories from Tony's over the years. I found these snippets with a quick search in my *Facebook* profile:

August 24, 2012: I went into Tony's Coffee Shop yesterday and asked what the special was for the day. They said if I sang my drink to them, they'd give me a quarter off. No biggy. I sang "Please give me a mocha for twenty-five cents off..." And everyone in the shop started applauding – so, of course, I gave a little bow – and they decided to give me 50 cents off because I was so spectacular. And then they told me no one else had sung for a drink all day!!! I'm pretty sure none of MY friends patronized Tony's Coffee Shop yesterday, right?

April 12, 2014: ... when I went to Tony's Coffee shop, the man in front of me (Al) paid for my mocha! So, of course, I paid for the coffee of the person behind me (Hannah), and she paid for the coffee of the person behind HER... and then I asked Al and Hannah to sign my copy of the Bellingham Review *(in which my photos are featured), and Al wrote: 'No matter where you are at any moment, love the moment you are in.' Which seemed the exactly right thing to write..."*

January 17, 2024

There's something very pleasing about watching snow drift outside the window while a fire burns in the woodstove and the Christmas lights sparkle in the window.

I bought a bouquet of purple roses on sale yesterday for $5.08 and they now sit in front of the tiny fake Christmas tree I haven't put away, yet. Little finches are hopping around in the snow on the deck, looking for seeds, while the cats watch them through our French doors.

I brought out a frozen bag of mixed fruit - mango chunks and blueberries and strawberries - and made a pie. I topped it with some whipped cream and ate it while the fruit was still warm from the oven.

I went for a walk through the 'hood and stopped for a moment to lift my face to the softly-falling snowflakes. The little wiener dog from across the street came scampering to me through snow that touched his belly, and I scratched him behind his ears and took his picture. He is an important part of my community.

After he scampered back to his home, I plopped into the snow in front of our house and made a snow angel.

Life's simple pleasures. Those precious moments that bring us magic.

Life is good.

January 29, 2024

Yesterday I was feeling kind of unchallenged. Bored. In real need of an adventure. No sooner had I put that thought out there, than my dear friend Rebecca messaged me to ask me if I'd like to join her on a drive up to Mount Baker.

Cosmic!

It was exactly the adventure I needed today. We took a walk in the snow at Heather Meadows and met a lovely Canadian woman named, coincidentally, Heather, who was enjoying a walk "oot" in the snow while her children and dad skied.

After we'd done a little exploring in the snow, Rebecca drove us back down the mountain and pulled us into the Silver Fir campground. She said she had something she wanted to show me. We walked for about ten minutes - past this cool old building built by the CCC back in the Great Depression - and then we were standing in front of a hollow tree with an entry hole. It was very cool. Rebecca darted inside and peeked out at me, and I followed her. It was snug and cozy in there. I felt like a little kid again, hiding out in the forest.

Rebecca drove us down to the Nooksack River then and we walked along the swollen, roiling river until a sign told us the trail was closed from that point on. A pile of fallen logs laying across the trail and into the river told the story.

Alpine air, roiling river, mossy maples, scampering squirrel, and a secret room in a tree. Magic!

February 5, 2024

For the last couple of months I've kept an eye out for one of my boardwalk friends, Beth, when I've been on my Bellingham walks. I wanted to give her a copy of my latest book, *Cosmic Kinship* - in which she and her pup, Wally, are featured in one of the chapters. But I never ran into her up there, and I was starting to fear I'd never see her again.

Today I went up for my walk on the boardwalk and ended up in the coffee shop at Boulevard Park. The young man who took my order was pretty fun. He asked me what I wanted and I found myself transfixed by the calories listed for each drink on the board behind him. "Wow. I don't think I've ever noticed the calories before," I said, and he started laughing. I finally decided on a vanilla latte and thanked him for his patience with me.

I sat down on a stool at one of those little tables that are, like, four feet off the floor - I like to sit on those stools and swing my legs back and forth like a little kid. I sat there sipping my latte and working on a *Wordle* puzzle and looking around at the other people in the shop with me. When I thought it was time to get going I started to put on my coat, and then I stopped - there was this woman sitting on a couch facing me - she'd been sitting there the whole time I was there - and it suddenly occurred to me that this woman looked an awful lot like Beth, the woman I'd been seeking for months! She was wearing a hat - which hid the top of her face a little bit - but...

I finished putting on my coat and walked up to her. "Beth?!" I asked. And it was her! I was so delighted to see her again. It seemed cosmic to me to find her right in front of me. I told her about the book I'd written, and she gave me her particulars so I could send her a copy.

Later in the day I took myself to a branch of my bank in Mount Vernon to cash a small check. I had such fun with the young teller behind the counter. He asked me my birthdate to verify I am who I am, and I gave him the month, day, and - opening my eyes really big to emphasize the absurdity of it! - my birth year. "Isn't that crazy? I was born in the last millennium!" He started laughing. "Yeah," I added, "When I was born there were no ATM machines."

He looked shocked. "What did you do?!" he asked. "Did you have to actually go into the banks to do everything?!"

I confirmed this. And then I told him that my dad had been born in (pause for dramatic effect) 1918! At the end of World War I. "He lived through The Great Depression, served in WWII, made it into *Wikipedia* for mountain climbing, and lived to be 101."

The teller looked suitably impressed by all this, and observed that my dad had lived a wonderful life.

Which he had.

I love people who let me have fun with them.

February 19, 2024

I ran into Kelly and Steve, the parents of two of my former eighth graders, in Fairhaven today. We chatted and laughed and talked about how cool it is that *FB* has helped us stay connected as our children have grown and married and we've become grandparents.

And then they brought me into the lobby of the Fairhaven Village Inn, where they'd spent the night. They had just checked out and couldn't take me up to a room, but they brought me into this cool room with a library and board games and a place where you could get drinks and food.

As we were standing in there, laughing and getting caught up, a hotel employee walked by with Kelly's clothes - Kelly'd forgotten them in the closet of their room! It was cosmic that we happened to be there in that moment when her clothes were being brought downstairs. And it was so fun to see Kelly and Steve again!

I went into the Colophon to treat myself to an African peanut soup and the hostess put me at my favorite table - the little table in the corner. I apologized to the two men sitting at the table next to me - our tables were pretty close together and I didn't want them to feel I was intruding on their space - but they assured me it was all good.

I puttered around on my phone for a while - trying to maintain boundaries with my table neighbors. I'm hard-of-hearing so I wouldn't have made a very good eavesdropper even if I'd wanted to be, but I enjoyed the cadence of their conversation, and the laughter. I could tell they were old friends.

When one of the men left to use the restroom, the other one turned to me and brought me into conversation. I don't think I'd fooled him by dinking around on my phone. I think he knew I'd been listening. I told him it sounded like he and his friend went way back, and shared history together - and he smiled and told me that his friend and he had met at WWU, like, 30 years ago and had stayed in contact all these years. I told him that was very cool - to have old friends who've known you for a big part of your life, and he agreed. His friend came back then and they both wished me a good day before they left.

One of the servers came by to ask me if I'd had my refill on my drink, yet, and I told them I had and I was happy. "I love this place," I told them. "Everyone is kind. And kindness is important."

The man sitting at the table across from me with his wife had been listening to my exchange with the server, and he nodded his head in agreement. He said kindness IS important. And he nodded his head again when I said that if you start with kindness, everything else flows from that.

I paid my check and wished the man and his wife a good day and they wished me the same.

Kindness makes everything better.

February 21, 2024

I didn't grow up with sisters, and I didn't birth daughters, so I rejoiced greatly when my sons married and their wives became part of our family.

My youngest son, Xander, and his wife, Kyla, live near us. I feel really blessed that they're close by and we're able to get together regularly. Kyla's good about reaching out to me and inviting me on lunch and movie dates – she seems to have an instinct for knowing when I most need to get out of the house and have a good laugh with her about life.

Last week Kyla invited me to go to her aunt's CreaviviTea shop (a tea and pottery shop in Bellingham) to have tea, and paint pottery with her. I had a lovely time painting a little ceramic fruit basket with strawberries and drinking Rooibos. And laughing, of course.

Yesterday Kyla messaged me to let me know our pottery was ready to pick up from the shop (it turned out great!), and afterwards we went out to lunch at our favorite Thai restaurant in Bellingham, Thai Maison. We talked (and laughed!) about friends and family, books and movies and television shows, and our world.

I love having young people in my life. And I love having people in my life who share my sense of humor. I think laughing out loud at the nonsense of life is one of the healthiest things we can do for ourselves.

March 1, 2024

Today was totally brimming with cosmic goodness.

Get this: I went into the supermarket this morning to pick up some stuff to help me organize my office better. I also thought I'd see if there were any bottles of "Knudsen's Just Blueberry" juice there - "Just Blueberry" has been on sale at the supermarket for a while, but the last several times I've checked the store's been out of stock. Today the "Just Blueberry" shelf appeared to be empty again, but there was a blueberry-pomegranate juice on the shelf below. I reached for a bottle of it, and when I pulled it out I peered behind it to see if... maybe... and there were three "Just Blueberry" bottles hidden behind it on the back of that shelf! I nabbed two of them for myself, and then put the third bottle where it should have been so someone else who was looking for it would find it waiting there - just for them! I pictured someone coming upon the last bottle of blueberry juice - on sale for $4.99! And I pictured that person smiling that they'd managed to find the last bottle.

Next I went in quest of pretzels. Lately I've been on a pretzel kick. And there are, like, a gazillion different types of pretzels! (Something you don't realize until you're on a pretzel kick.) There was a man stocking the shelves in the pretzel aisle and I asked him what his favorite kind of pretzel is. Cosmically, I'd asked the just right person! This man knew everything about pretzels - shapes, tastes, sizes. He told me his favorites are actually the pretzel chips - which, he told me, could be found down there - near the deli - just behind that woman getting oranges. And then he said he was on his way to stock something down there - so I just followed in his wake. I was in pretzel heaven. He yelled across to me from the other side of the shelves where I was standing, that there were even more pretzels on the other side. I think he was as excited to share his knowledge of pretzels with me as I was to receive it. I ended up with a very fine bag of pretzel chips - found thanks to the help of the man I shall heretofore refer to as "Pretzel Man."

After the supermarket, I stopped at a Starbucks near I-5 for a mocha. As I was sitting at my table, drinking my mocha and scrolling through *FB*, I came upon a *Harry Potter* meme, courtesy of my irreverent Humoristian friend, Admiralissimo Ben, that had me, literally, laughing out loud. I had to share this with someone. A young couple (I'm guessing from Canada) had just come in and had seated themselves at the table next to me. I leaned over and asked if I could share this *FB* thing with them - because I had to share it with someone. They grinned and agreed, so I showed them the meme and they both started laughing, too. When I got up to leave, I thanked them for letting me share, and we all wished each other a good day.

Later I went to Michaels craft store to pick up a frame for one of my dad's watercolors. And there was a frame sale going on! The sign said if I bought one frame, I could get two more for free! It seemed too good to be true, but I grabbed three frames and brought them down to the cashier to see if I'd read the sign right. And I had! Three frames for the price of one! Wowza!

I ended my shopping spree with an impulsive stop at See's Candy. When I walked in everyone was looking very serious. And I said, "Shouldn't everyone be smiling here? We're in a chocolate shop!" The other customers laughed and agreed with me. I found out that a pair of them were celebrating their 32nd anniversary near the end of the month - and I told them that my 40th anniversary is at the end of the month! "I've been married longer than I was single!" I said. "Whoah." And we all "whoah"ed at the idea of that.

It is the end of a cosmic day. My office is organized; Dad's watercolor is framed and hanging on a wall; I've met some very cool people today; and I'm nestled in the comfy chair with a glass of "Just Blueberry" juice. Life is good.

March 12, 2024

My son, Andrew, and his wife, Christina, and my grandbaby, Linh, arrived from Australia last week, and will be spending the summer with us. Kyla and Xander came over today to meet their little niece for the first time, and to reunite with Andrew and Christina – whom they hadn't seen in a year.

My heart is so full and happy to have everyone close again!

I bought a children's music kit this morning for Linh – it has a tambourine, a couple of maracas, a triangle, a clapper, and a set of cymbals. After we'd all settled into the living room to converse and get caught up, Andrew thought to fetch the instruments and hand them out to us. Pretty soon we were sitting in a circle on the living room floor, making spontaneous "music" for Linh - who sat in the middle of the circle with one of the maracas, fascinated by what we were up to.

My family is crazy fun.

And I'm still grinning.

March 17, 2024

We took the baby on her inaugural walk on the boardwalk today. And oh, my friends, it was magic!

There were babies everywhere! It was so fun to connect with the other parents and grandparents and show off our wee ones to each other.

Robert, from the Whatcom Association of Celestial Observers, was there with his humongo telescope, doing some volunteer work for NASA. He let folks look at the moon through his telescope, and let everyone know about the lunar eclipse coming up on April 8th. (I snapped a quick photo of the moon through his lens.)

We ran into Natalie, an old friend of Andrew's, on the boardwalk, and they were with a chap named Blake, who I'm pretty sure was a celebrity in disguise. His shoes gave him away – he was definitely wearing celebrity shoes – they were dressy-looking with leather toes and tan canvas over the arch. Those shoes gave him away, and I let Blake know that. He started cracking up.

As we were coming back up the ramp from Taylor Dock we met Sukhman and Gurkirat, arrayed in the beautiful purple robes that families of Sikh priests are allowed to wear. Sukhman and Gurkirat graciously posed for me and allowed me to take their picture.

Not far past Sukhman and Gurkirat, we came upon Aaron, an American gymnast and dancer who competed internationally with a Canadian gymnastics team. Aaron stopped to ask about Christina's accent – he guessed correctly that her accent is Australian. Aaron said Australian accents were his favorite. He and Andrew and Christina talked for a bit about their recent travels to Japan – they all agreed Japan is a beautiful, clean, polite country – and amazingly quiet for such a populous place.

Our day ended with a glorious sunset! Magic!

March 22, 2024

This amazing thing happened today. Yesterday, the daughter of one of Dad's old climbing buddies invited me to her house to gift me with some of her dad's old mountaineering mementos - things that were connected to MY dad in some way. I brought everything out to my car and drove home. When I got home, I decided to just leave the mementos on the front passenger seat of the car until I could find the right place for them in the house.

So this morning I ran some errands, and then, when I got home, I glanced over at the mementos on my front seat and my eyes landed on the corner of an autographed American Alpine Club photo. And I did a double-take. What the...?!!! There was my friend Deidre's autograph - right above her husband Andrew's!

What makes this so remarkable is that Deidre isn't among the people that I associate with mountaineering or my dad. Deidre is a friend I met years ago - I think on one of my walks. I knew her husband, Andrew, was a climber, but I never knew there was a connection with my dad.

And what was further remarkable was that Deidre was coming over to my house tonight for our annual Women's Peace Fellowship gathering!! It was another one of those times in my life when it felt like the Cosmos had given me a gift and was celebrating with me. When Deidre arrived for the meeting tonight, I shared the photo with her - and we both rejoiced in the cosmic coincidence of it.

Our Women's Peace Fellowship gathering was wonderful. I'm still glowing with the love and hope that filled my home. I have a remarkable group of friends: musicians, writers, teachers, artists. The women who come to my fellowship gatherings all have heart and wisdom, and they always leave me feeling inspired. This year, in addition to the nine friends who joined me for our gathering,

Andrew and Christina, and seven-month-old Linh, were here with us, too. It felt so good to have my house brimming with family and friends tonight.

We gathered in a circle around the dining-room table and took turns sharing words of inspiration – quotes and poems, essays, and stories - with each other. Then my friend, Tracy Spring, brought out her guitar and gave us a concert in my living room. It was a beautiful finish to a lovely night.

Bev and Carmen and Claudia, Dahli and Dawn and Deidre, Paula, Peggy, Rebecca, Rosemary, and Tracy are all dear to me – an important part of my community, and an important part of our world. They know how to love.

April 21, 2024

A year ago a woman from the Skagit Unitarian Universalist Fellowship contacted me to invite me to present the sermon today. I'd spoken at the SUUF three times before – twice in person, and once, during the Pandemic, via *Zoom*. I was happy to be invited back to speak today. I always have such fun with the SUUF folks. It's like a comedy club there – everyone knows how to laugh. This group of people has, also, always been kind to me. I looked forward to seeing them all again.

I always get nervous before I present my sermon – afraid I'm going to goof up. "Stage jitters" I guess is what you'd call it. On the drive to the fellowship hall I was almost beside myself with "stage jitters." But once Scott parked the car and we were greeted by our first UU members, I felt the jitters just melt away. I knew it was going to be okay. I was with my people.

I spoke with the celebrant about the order of the service, where I should sit, and when I should go up to the platform. And George – who is the fellowship's highly intelligent and wonderfully affable techno wizard – showed me how the audiotaping would work, and pointed out the Zoom camera to me so I would know where to look to include the people who were watching from their homes.

Then I had a look around the hall – went to their bulletin board to see what they were up to, and found a memorial wall to members who had passed on. I found the name of a beloved friend on that wall – Peggy Bissell.

Peggy was one of the most courageous and honest women I've ever known. I met her when I ran for school board in 2019. She'd contacted me to interview me – to find out for herself who I was. And she wasn't afraid to ask the questions that were important to her. She didn't beat around the bush. Once our interview was done, she became my champion – spreading the word that I was the one people should vote for. I made it past the primary, but lost to the incumbent in the general election. (I thanked the incumbent profusely for winning! I can't imagine how challenging it would have been to serve on a school board during the Pandemic.) And Peggy Bissell became one of my dearest friends. I teared up when I saw her name on the SUUF memorial wall.

The topic of my sermon was "The Healing Power of Love" – a topic I'd used the first time I'd spoken at the hall. And as I spoke about the power of Love, I could feel the love being reflected back to me by the congregation. The whole room glowed with Love. It was beautiful.

I'm so grateful for every opportunity we have to share inspiration and hope and kindness with one another. I'm so grateful to the SUUF Fellowship for inviting me to speak today.

May 2, 2024

So, as you know, one of the books I published last year was *Cosmic Kinship* - a book about the new friends I meet on my adventures, and the kinship we all have with one another (a sequel to *Cosmic Connections* published a couple years ago). Two of the people I mention in *Cosmic Kinship* are Jim and Shiva - a couple I sometimes connect with on the Bellingham boardwalk. I've been carrying around a copy of the book in my little backpack, hoping to run into them on the boardwalk so's I could give it to them.

I started carrying it around with me a few weeks ago. The first day I had it with me, I didn't run into Jim and Shiva, but I ran into another person featured in the book, Cash, and ended up giving it to him instead. And I realized then that THAT copy was meant for him. I was glad I had the book with me so I could give it to him.

The week after that I ran into Jim three times on the boardwalk - but, alas, I hadn't replaced the copy I'd given to Cash, and didn't have one to give to Jim.

This week I decided to try again. I stuffed another copy of *Cosmic Kinship* in my backpack and set out for the boardwalk. And, again, things didn't turn out as I envisioned, but I think they turned out the way they were meant to.

I went into the coffee shop at Boulevard Park to get myself a mocha. My friend, Beth (also featured in *Cosmic Kinship*), was in front of me in line and Brandon, the barista, was getting her set up in the new points system at the coffee shop. Brandon had helped me with this the day before (I basically handed him my phone and let him push the buttons - and presto shazaam! I was officially in the system!). I told Beth she was doing great, and she grinned. (Boomers unite!)

When I got up to the counter, Brandon asked me what I was taking photos of "today." I held up my camera and pointed it at him and told him (click!), "You." He started laughing, passing my "people with a sense of humor" test.

I ran into Cash again at the coffee shop. Cash is one of those people that always puts a smile on my face - and, in the course of our conversation yesterday, I learned that he, too, is an author! (Cash is the author of *Eight Leader Types in the White House.*) I also learned that he narrates audiobooks and is appearing in a play soon. How cool is that?!

I did not, however, run into Jim and Shiva yesterday.

After my walk on the Bellingham boardwalk, I didn't feel I was done with my adventures for the day, yet, so I drove to La Conner to pay my broadband bill. I always look forward to seeing Jolyne and Jeri at the broadband office - I know I can count on them to make me laugh. They are a comedy team. (They are in my book, too!)

After I'd paid my broadband bill I walked along the La Conner boardwalk to the Calico Cupboard. I bought some cookies (I planned to bring a couple back to Jolyne and Jeri on my way back to the car), and then decided to stay and have some brunch there.

My server at the Calico Cupboard, Kala, was (surprise!) another person I wrote about in *Cosmic Kinship*. Kala is one of those joyful people who makes the world a better place just by existing. She remembered me as soon as she saw me and let me know that the book I'd dropped off at the Calico Cupboard for her last year had never made it into her hands.

Whoah. I let Kala know that I happened to have a copy of my book with me, and that I'd just realized it was meant for her. She grinned a big grin and asked me if I would sign it for her. I wrote: "For Kala - thank you for your joy!"

So I went back to the boardwalk today with yet ANOTHER copy of my book in my backpack. I ran into Cash again - that was fun. And when I walked into the coffee shop I saw it was manned by the same delightful baristas from the day before. "Are you guys still here?!" I asked. And they started laughing.

There was a young man cleaning the windows of the shop, and I snapped a couple pictures of him through the window-cleaning suds. He was a good sport about my antics and, when I came outside to ask him if I could use his photo on *Facebook*, he graciously agreed to this and introduced himself as Aidan.

On the way back to my car I remet a little pup I'd met yesterday. Tucker's human let me scratch little Tucker behind the ears and snap a photo. A little later I met another new pup-friend, Princess Buttercup, who came up and sniffed my hand and let me rub her back. Her human gave me permission to take a photo of her sweet face.

When I got back to my car, I realized I needed some more walking and decided to do some exploring on the trails that sprout out from Fairhaven Park. I've never really done much exploring there and wasn't sure where the trail was going to take me, but I ran into two helpful gents, Mike and Steve, who explained where I was, and where I was going, and where I'd end up at the end. Basically, I was on a small loop.

When I got back to Fairhaven Park, I met ANOTHER new pup-friend, 14-year-old Dotty. Dotty, her human explained to me, had recently become deaf. But Dotty could tell I was a friend and turned to me and came up to me for a pet on the head. Such a sweetie!

I shall return soon to the boardwalk, in my continuing quest for Jim and Shiva. They're bound to turn up some day, right?

May 8, 2024

I imagine Mom tucking me into bed and asking me about my day. And I tell her…

I took the grandbaby out into the sunshine on the back deck and sat in a chair and she bounced on my lap for a while. We listened to the birds singing and she put her forehead against mine and chatted to me in her own language about life, and we laughed and sang together, and celebrated being alive on this fine spring day.

After she and my son and daughter-in-law left to run errands, I put *Four Weddings and a Funeral* on TV in the background while I washed the dishes and cleaned the counter and answered emails and worked on my *Blossoms* word game.

Then I went to the post office and got my mail and, just before I left, Luciano, a Neopolitan Mastiff, stuck his head out of the truck that pulled into the space next to me. Luciano and I are new friends – I just met him for the first time a couple of days ago – and I was so happy to see him again. I got out of my car to say hi to him. His kind human recognized me and gave me a biscuit to feed Luciano. I held it out on a flat palm to feed him in the same way I would feed a horse. He sucked up the biscuit and left a trail of doggy slobber on my hand. It was awesome.

I drove from the post office to the supermarket to pick up some things before I headed home. The older woman in front of me in the checkout line was classy and elegant looking. She had golden open-toed sandals, tan capris, and sparkly, spangly jewelry, and her hair was beautifully coiffed in what we used to call a "page boy." She turned to smile at me and to apologize for taking so long to put her stuff on the counter, and I told her I loved her shoes and her earrings and… oh look! We had the same kind of reusable shopping bags! She laughed and said she thought she'd gotten hers from some charity she'd donated to. I looked at the bottom of my bag and saw that I'd gotten it from the Lakota Sioux people – a group I donate to regularly. I'd forgotten I'd gotten that bag from them. It was cool to realize this gracious put-together woman and I both donate to the same people. I love making connections like that.

I stopped at the Edison Cafe to get some lunch and a raspberry Italian soda and sat at the table outside to wait. Soon Austin (the owner of the cafe and one of my former eighth graders) delivered the soda to me. He'd topped the soda with whipped cream and sprinkles. It was beautiful.

Before I'd come outside, I'd nodded and smiled to a couple of young men eating their lunch at a table inside – one of them was covered in tattoo art, and the other had a long black braid past his waist. The thought came to me that I would love to have been the teacher to these gentle giants – they both emanated kindness and good will. When they came out to get in their car, they smiled at me again and wished me a good day, and I wished them one, too. I felt the genuineness of their wish for me, and our new connection.

I came home and mowed the lawn in the front of the house and in my Secret Garden and immersed myself in the joys of spring: the smell of freshly-mowed grass; the birdsong; the sun shining on my face. It was just lovely.

I watched a movie I found on *Netflix* (*The Peanut Butter Falcon*) and then my son and daughter-in-law came home, and my other daughter-in-law stopped by – and it was so joy-filled to have everyone in the house, laughing and sharing space.

Then baby Linh bounced on my lap and chatted to me for a while about her day, and I nodded at her insightful comments, and told her I love her.

It has been a good day, Mom.

May 9, 2024

At the beginning of my Bellingham walk today I met a new friend, Tony, owner of Mokka Toni's. What an interesting young man! While he put together an exotic coffee for me with energy from the solar panels attached to his van, I learned all sorts of cool things: Tony had taught English for a year in Japan, and I learned that when you address someone in Japanese you make sure to add "San" after their name; and if you're asking a question, you add "ka" at the end of a sentence to show it's a question. I learned one of Tony's ancestors was a Buffalo soldier, and that his ancestry included Mexican, Cherokee (he's descended from people who were on the Trail of Tears), and Spanish. I learned that he named his coffee stand after his mom, Toni, because, as he said, he's "a mamma's boy," and I learned that his grandmother gave him the name "storyteller" at the end of her life because Tony, she said, sure likes to talk. Tony was fun, and I'm really glad I got to meet him today. He also makes a really good cup of coffee.

I met a new pup friend today, too. Little Kekoa (Kekoa's human told me that "Kekoa" means "warrior" in Hawaiian) saw me coming from yards away, and gave me a smile. Kekoa kept smiling as I scratched him behind the ears and moved closer to me so I could pet his back, too.

There were some trail maintenance workers trimming the hedge that grows alongside the boardwalk trail (Tyler gave me the "thumbs up" to take his picture while he trimmed). Soon I saw Jillian, a florist, with an armful of the trimmings – she was so excited – she said she was going to use the trimmings in a Mother's Day bouquet for her mom.

As I was coming back down the boardwalk I stopped for a quick chat with a cheery young woman who agreed with me that on sunny days like this in western Washington, it's almost criminal not to be outside. She said she'd made sure to get some sunshine before she had to start work in a couple hours.

I passed Tony again on my way back to the car and wished him a good day, and he smiled and wished me the same.

May 14, 2024

Let me introduce you to Kay. I met Kay on my walk to Boulevard Park this week and she had a story to tell. It started with a joke:

She pointed to a dog and said, "What if I told you that that dog can jump higher than this tree?" (She pointed to a large tree next to the path.) And then she asked, "Have you ever seen that tree jump?"

Then Kay expanded on her story. Apparently, she'd been down at Taylor Dock one time and had seen a man walking a dog. He was a little grumpy, and when she told him his dog could jump higher than that three-story building, the man had made clear that it wasn't HIS dog - it belonged to his son, but his son never walked it, so HE had to. "Okay… but…" Kay had replied, and then returned to her joke. "This dog can jump higher than that three-story building." (Pause.) "Have you ever seen that building jump?" she asked the grumpy man.

He said, "I haven't lived here that long."

May 18, 2024

It has been a week, my friends. One of those our-internet-disconnects-just-as-I'm-about-to-email-off-important-papers weeks. One of those the-clothes-dryer-kicks-the-bucket-just-after-we've-loaded-it-with-wet-clothes-that-have-been-sitting-in-the-washer-all-day weeks. One of those my-cellphone-didn't-charge-during-the-night-but-I-didn't-notice-until-I-was-already-running-errands weeks. Things have been just a little bit off here.

On the other hand…

I stopped and got a mocha at the coffee shop in Boulevard Park and sat at one of those high tables again, so I could swing my legs.

Not long after I sat there, a couple sat at the high table next to me. There was a great energy coming from this couple – they were enjoying each other and listening to each other and they were smart and funny. I figured they were on a date. When I heard the words "teach" and "engineering" and "higher level thinking," my ears perked up and I shamelessly listened in – I was a teacher; my oldest son got his degree in mechanical engineering; and who doesn't like "higher level thinking," right?! Finally, I confessed to the couple that I'd been eavesdropping.

I had such fun getting to know Jeremy and Emily! I told them I hadn't wanted to intrude into their conversation because it looked like they were on a date. They started laughing and said they'd actually been married ten years! I learned they now live in San Francisco, and are up here to visit their friend who owns a restaurant in Bellingham. I told them my youngest son and his wife had owned a restaurant in Bellingham, too, for a while – and we talked for a bit about the challenges of restaurant ownership. Jeremy is an engineer now, but at one point he'd been a science teacher – and we shared our teaching stories.

I told Emily and Jeremy about "The Seeing Bellingham" group on *Facebook*, and how I like to share stories and pictures there about the cool people I meet in Bellingham. I asked them if I could post a picture of THEM there, and they graciously agreed to pose for me.

It has been a week, my friends. One of those I-met-cool-new-people-in-Bellingham weeks! One of those I-happen-to-check-*Facebook*-and-find-my-friend-Tracy-is-going-to-be-performing-in-La Conner-in-an-hour-and-my-schedule-is-free weeks! One of those I-ran-into-my-dear-friend-Rebecca-and-her-sweet-pup-Bear-on-the-boardwalk weeks! One of those look-at-all-the-purple-flowers-of-May weeks!

May 19, 2024

Scott and I went hiking on the Baker Lake Trail today. The bridge over Anderson Creek had been washed away, and people were either crossing over a log across the river, or fording it. The people who used the log said it was waaay safer than trying to ford. The people who forded said it was waaay safer than trying to cross on the log. The people who had already crossed logs and forded rivers in earlier chapters in their lives realized there was actually a third option in THIS chapter of their lives: Sit on big boulders by the creek and eat trail mix and listen to the riversong and then head back through the ferny fairy forest.!

Today was brimming with magic: trilliums and bleeding heart flowers; tree trunks big enough to fit a tiny house in; little brooks singing past ferns and moss and mushrooms; and the waterfalls of Anderson Creek.

It was a lovely day for a hike. (What day ISN'T a lovely day for a hike?)

May 21, 2024

Honestly, I was feeling pretty down today – dismayed at the direction the world seems to be headed; and disappointed in myself, too – feeling like I could have been a better mother, wife, daughter, teacher, friend, in my life.

The thought came to me to get out of the house and find a quiet corner somewhere where I could do some self-reflection and have an internal conversation with the Cosmos.

When I started out I wasn't sure where I was going to end up, exactly – but as I followed the nudgings of the Cosmos I found myself at Pacioni's in Mount Vernon. I sat in a booth in the back and ordered a half a veggie panini, listened to the soft background music and the sounds of friends talking and laughing. Watched the rain drizzling outside the front window.

I realized I missed Mom. I thought about how I could always tell her what was in my heart – and she never judged me or my words. She always saw the best in me. I missed that.

When I was done with my panini and had paid, I tidied up my table, put on my coat, and started for the door.

And this is when I saw that two of my favorite people had been sitting in there, eating their lunch, too! We all gave each other hugs and talked about children and grandchildren and the state of the world, and how we maybe can't change the big things in the world, but we can be kind to the people in our community, the people with whom we come in contact. I told them they are two of the people that do this really well – and then they said *I* did this! They said I was the perfect example of this! They said they'd been talking to one of my former students a while ago and my name had come up in the conversation and my former student had said that EVERYone should have a Karen Terrell for a teacher.

I teared up. I stood there, in front of my friends, and I teared up. They had no idea the gift they'd just given me – it was the exactly right thing I needed to hear just then. To know that someone thought I'd made a difference – to know that someone thought I'd done something right in my life – this was huge for me.

And I realized that the mother-love I'd been missing was right there with me – being expressed to me by my beautiful friends.

The Cosmos led me exactly where I needed to be today.

May 31, 2024

Magic, my friends! On my walk on the Bellingham boardwalk this morning, a gentleman noticed I was taking photos of a heron on the beach and told me all about the trees near the dog park that are filled with herons and their nests. I went to take a look and found magic there.

There were dozens of heron nests in the trees – each filled with two or three little tuft-headed baby herons. And periodically the papa and mama herons would swoop into the nests and feed their squawking nestlings.

I snapped some pictures for a while, and then went home and told Scott I had some magic to show him. We drove back up to Bellingham together and hiked into the rookery. I enjoyed seeing the expression on his face when he saw what I had seen a couple of hours before. He saw the magic.

We spent the next half hour taking photos and witnessing this miracle of nature together.

June 5, 2024

I decided to head up to Bellingham early this morning for a quick walk on the boardwalk to start my day. There were clumps of traffic along the way and I decided to exit at Nulle Road to avoid what was going on through that narrow corridor on I-5 that runs above Lake Samish.

When I exited and turned left, I saw that there was a road crew with detour signs and stop signs waiting just ahead of me. I was momentarily confused by this and turned on the road just before the road crew. But just as I turned I saw "STOP" and "DO NOT ENTER" signs and realized that I'd just turned into an off-ramp from I-5. I was going the wrong direction!

I stopped immediately to back up and, as I did this, a young man from the road crew ran out, waving his arms - he'd seen what I was about to do, too - and looked like he was willing to throw himself in front of my car to stop me from killing myself and other people. He was a hero. I rolled down my window, laughing at myself, and thanked him, and he started laughing, too, and said he'd seen me start up the ramp and was thinking. "No way!!!" I backed my car off the ramp, and the young man and I smiled and waved to each other as I went past him, going the RIGHT direction this time.

For about a month now I've been carrying my book, *Cosmic Kinship*, around in my purse in the hope that I would run into Jim and Shiva on the boardwalk and could give them a copy. But I have not seen them and was starting to give up hope I ever would. Today, though, I stopped on the boardwalk to take pictures of the boats bobbing around on the bay and glanced up to smile at a man who was passing me - and found myself looking at Jim! Oh, happy day! I dug out my copy of the book, signed it, and handed it to him. Jim thanked me and told me he'd be sure to let Shiva see it, too.

I got to Boulevard Park and sat on a bench and toodled around on my phone for a while, glancing up every now and then to watch the people and pups and birds. On one of my glances I spotted Kay - a woman I'd met a couple weeks ago. I let her know that I'd posted her picture on *Facebook* and that she had a fan club - one person had commented on my post that Kay was her neighbor and she loved her. Another commenter said that she loved Kay, too, and that Kay always started her conversations with a good joke. Kay started laughing then, and said if I kept telling her this stuff her head might get too big to fit in the car.

I started back to my car then, taking photos as I went. And it occurred to me that if I'd continued in the wrong direction up that off-ramp I might not have been there to finally give my book to Jim, or to re-connect with Kay in Boulevard Park.

Whoah.

June 7, 2024

Kyla texted me yesterday to see if we could meet up today in Bellingham. In a cool coincidence, I happened to be gifting Christina some time at the Blessings Salon Spa today (Christina hasn't had much time to splurge on herself since becoming a mum). I invited Kyla to join me in taking little Linh out for a stroll on the boardwalk while her mum got her hair styled. Kyla loves being Linh's aunty and happily agreed to join her little niece and me on the boardwalk.

We had such fun taking turns proudly pushing Linh in her stroller. We met other babies in strollers, and puppies on leashes, and, just as we were heading back to the spa to meet up again with Christina, Linh closed her eyes and fell asleep. Is there anything more peaceful than a sleeping baby?

Christina, Kyla, and I decided to go to lunch at J's Kitchen, the new Puerto Rican restaurant in Fairhaven. It was so lovely to be with "the girls" again – laughing together, and enjoying Linh as she babbled and grinned, and nibbled on Puerto Rican food

At one point a mother with a toddler a little older than Linh came into the restaurant, and pretty soon Linh and this little boy had crawled up to each other across the restaurant and were checking each other out. The little boy squatted in front of Linh, his hands folded in front of him like a grown-up, and smiled at Linh, and she blinked back at him. It was very dear.

These are precious times.

June 8, 2024

Today Christina and I took baby Linh to Deception Pass for some beach time.

I had a mini life-lesson while I was there. I was on the hunt for agates, of course - but was not having much success with finding any. I told Christina that maybe today I needed to not have any goals about finding agates, or hiking down as far as that point on the beach or anything. She asked, "So your goal today is to not have any goals?" Which made me start cracking up. She offered the suggestion that maybe I should just let go of all goals - and I felt the tension lift from my shoulders.

So here's what happened: I did not find any agates, but I did find this really pretty rock that sparkled in the sun with tiny crystals; and I made friends with a happy pup named Koda; and we met these chaps named James and Mike who had a *Dr. Who* sticker on their car, and who waved and smiled at Baby Linh and patiently let me brag to them about being a grandma.

And then *this* happened: There was this piece of driftwood floating on the water about ten yards out and a couple next to me was trying to hit the driftwood with rocks. They didn't seem to be having much success with this. When the driftwood floated in front of me, I figured it was MY turn to try to hit it with rocks. But I didn't have much success with it, either, and - seeing as how it was a day for no goals - I just let it move past me, and continued with my search for rocks. I found a nice flat one and skipped it across the water. It only skipped twice before it plopped in and sank - but that was okay. Then I glanced down the beach and noticed that the tide had brought in the driftwood I'd been trying to hit with rocks. So I walked down the beach, picked up a rock, and dropped it onto the driftwood. To paraphrase some famous saying, "If the rock will not come to the driftwood, the driftwood will come to the rock."

It was fun watching little Linh get acquainted with surf, sand and seaweed. We kept a careful watch on her because everything went instantly to her mouth – but I enjoyed watching her explore and study things that were new to her. Christina is a wonderful mum – very patient and kind - and it brought me joy to watch her interactions with Linh. I took pictures of Christina wading into the water with Linh on her hip, and took more pictures of her stretched out in the sun with Linh, soaking in the rays. Peace!

There were other young families there, exploring the shore and picnicking. Linh is fascinated with other babies. I've noticed that when babies get close to each other they look directly into each other's eyes – trying to figure out what they're looking at, maybe. It's completely disarming.

We had a lovely time at the beach, soaking in the sunshine, and breathing in the briny air, and just be-ing. With no goals.

June 9, 2024

Let me tell you about my 'hood: Three of my former eighth graders live on the Bow loop - Brooke and her family live across the street on the left, Mike and his family live across the street on the right, and Brock and his family live on the other side of the loop. Our new neighbors, Ali and Devin, live in the house between Mike and Brooke, with their two little girls, Beatrix and Clementine. Clementine is just a couple months older than Linh, and it's been so fun watching the toddlers get to know each other.

On the other side of Brooke is Lucy. Lucy is originally from Ireland and taught English at Skagit Valley College until she retired a couple years ago. Lucy was diagnosed with cancer five years ago and given just months to live, but she decided she wasn't ready to die, yet, and here she is. I told her to just keep breathing and she laughed and agreed that that's the key.

Further down the loop are Ginny and Cameron with their three youngsters. Paul, a musician and retired postal worker from Wisconsin, lives in the last house before you leave the loop. Brenda and Tracy live in a house with a clear view all the way down the street we live on – and, seeing as how they're both retired Army military police officers, we think it's kind of nice to have them keeping an eye out on things for us.

Fellow Boomers, Diana and Robert, live next door to us and have created a magical space with gardens and hanging baskets, a stone patio and a greenhouse. More Boomers, Jeff and Mary Anne, live on the other side of Diana and Robert. Jeff is a retired Air Force officer, and Mary Anne is one of those neighbors that's always the first person to appear when you need help. Around the corner you'll find Diane – who invited me over to use her crafts and sewing room when she learned I was going through a clinical depression, and showered me with her unending kindness. Linda lives in the house across from Diane, and recently lost her brother, who shared the house with her, to cancer. I always wave when I go by her house – just to let her know I'm here if she needs me.

Lulu and Barry live next to Diane, and their daughter, Jenny, and their grandchildren live in the house across from them. I rarely see Lulu or Jenny without welcoming smiles on their faces, and I often pass Lulu when we're both taking walks around the 'hood. Sue lives down the street from Lulu and always stops what she's doing and takes time to chat with me when I'm walking past her house. Behind Sue's house is Gary and Nancy's house. Gary and Nancy let us take pictures of the sunset from their big field – and when Scott and I discovered the Northern Lights glowing over Bow, I knocked on Gary and Nancy's door, and Nancy joined us in their field to marvel with us at the magic. Next to Gary and Nancy are Teresa and Pat. Teresa worked for years as a teacher's aide in the school where I taught, and Pat went through knee surgery about the same time Scott did a couple years ago.

Dahli bought the old church in our neighborhood and is fixing it up as a place to live and maybe put on concerts. Paula lives next to the church and can often be seen taking her grandchildren on walks. Tyler and Dana live a couple houses down the street from Paula, with their little girl, Esther – whom I've had the joy of watching grow from a newborn to a lively three-year-old. And Ron, who is a retired teacher like me, lives across from Tyler and Dana.

These are the people of our little Bow community – the people we might meet when we take Linh for a walk around the loop in her stroller, or when we're outside working in the yard. We know each other and we look out for each other. I feel really blessed to live in this neighborhood.

June 15, 2024

We arrived in Pennsylvania a couple of days ago to celebrate my mother-in-law Marilyn's 95th birthday. Linh is our grandbaby's Vietnamese nickname for "Marilyn" – Linh was named after her great-grandma. I've been looking forward to the two Marilyns finally meeting in the person, and, when they finally did, it was everything I'd hoped for! Little Linh crawled around her great-grandma's chair and peeked up at her, and Great-Grandma Marilyn leaned over and smiled down at her. Soon Linh was in Marilyn's lap, and they were smiling at each other and getting acquainted.

Marilyn's birthday party was today at her faith home, the Grove City Methodist Church. Oh, it was so fun! I finally met Bernice, one of my *Facebook* friends, in person and we gave each other hugs. All Scott's sisters and their husbands were there – Marla and Dave; Bev and Matt; and Lori and Bill – and their children and grandchildren were there, too.

Watching baby Linh playing with her young cousins in the church's gymnasium was a hoot. Though she was the youngest one on the gym floor, she wasn't shy at all and crawled-toddled right up to her older cousins to play in their games. Her older cousins were very good about including her in their play and protecting her from bouncing balls. I enjoyed watching their interactions with 11-month-old Linh.

It's been so good to be with the Terrells again. I wish we all lived closer together so we could spend more time with each other. As I've mentioned before, I didn't grow up with sisters. But when I married Scott, one of the many cool things that happened was that I automatically had three new sisters to call my own. I'm really grateful for their kinship.

June 22, 2024

I planned on taking a quick hike around Lake Padden today, but there was a triathlon happening there, so I found myself heading towards Fairhaven instead. Once I got to Fairhaven, I felt myself pulled to the heron rookery again. It had been more than a week since I'd been to the rookery, and I wanted to see how the fledglings were doing. The rookery is a sacred place - full of new life just beginning, and I'm glad I went there today.

When I left the rookery and was heading back to my car, I noticed a woman and her pup friends crouched next to a fence - they appeared to be looking for something. I asked the woman, Sue, what she was looking for, and she said that Teddy and Pepper's ball had rolled under the fence into the bushes and she and the pups were trying to find it. Teddy and Pepper looked determined to find their tennis ball - sniffing for it, and trying to dig their way under the fence - and I determined that I would help them.

Sue said it would help to have a stick.   I looked around and saw a stick that might do the trick. I used it to push back some of the branches on the other side of the fence and found the ball waiting for us a couple of feet from the fence. I handed the stick to Sue and she slowly maneuvered the ball up close enough to the fence that she could reach her hand under and pull it out. Success! The pups were so happy to have their ball back!

Being able to help Teddy and Pepper totally made my day.

July 1, 2024

This morning Baby Linh raced up to me on all fours, pulled herself
up on a basket next to my chair and looked at me with a big grin on
her face. Then she started laughing. She laughed and laughed a big
rolling belly laugh mixed with happy squeals for a good three
minutes. And I laughed with her. We laughed just for the sheer joy
of laughing. It was the most therapeutic three minutes I had all day.

Forehead to forehead,
nose to nose, and grin to grin,
Grandbaby reaches out
and squeezes my nose.

This is happiness.

she points at me
like a celebrity
on the red carpet
and grins her sweet grin
then toddles to me
and reaches her arms up for me
to lift her onto my hip
we go out to the deck
and sit in the sunshine
and I sing to her an old Beatles ballad:
"Who knows how long I've loved you…?"
and she bops her head to the beat
and then rests
her head on my chest
and I melt with the sweetness of it

July 3, 2024

It has been a challenging week – both personally and globally, I guess – and I needed to get out and exchange smiles and meet new friends and see the good in the world.

As I was on my way to Fred Meyer's yesterday, I realized that it was "Senior Day" there and I'd get to buy things with a discount. So that was cool. I love Senior Day at Fred Meyer's – not just because of the discount, but because it's kind of fun to be with a store full of other people who were alive when the Beatles first appeared on Ed Sullivan, and when man took his first steps on the moon. There's a kinship there.

As I was checking out, I had to keep asking the cashier to repeat herself, and we both started laughing. I commended her for her patience with me, and with the other seniors there. I told her my dad lived to be 101 and I was his POA at the end and, maybe because of this, I can recognize in other people the ones who care for, and know HOW to care for, our society's oldest members. The cashier laughed and said she told her older relations they don't need to worry, she's got their backs.

I also met some way cool "youngsters" at Fred's yesterday – and by youngsters, I mean young people around my sons' ages – late twenties and early thirties.

I'd stopped in the photo department to buy photo paper and ink and there was a young man in the aisle, looking for computer stuff, I think,   He had this amazing hair – curly and long and red and tied up in a ponytail. I turned to him and said, "It has to be said: You have amazing hair." He started laughing and thanked me. He told me that he's the only one in his family who ended up with curly hair – and he didn't get his until he was twelve or so. I told him the same was true for my eldest son.

Later, as I was waiting in line at the in-store Starbucks, I got into conversation with two young families with babies in carts ahead of me in the line. The mother of one of the babies said that the babies were cousins and were only a few months apart in age – and I learned the youngest was only two weeks older than my granddaughter. So that was pretty cool. I got into conversation with the father of one of the babies and learned he was my oldest son's age. And, as we stood in line at the Starbucks in Fred's, he talked to me about his recent spiritual journey, and the importance of the sun, and the connection he feels with nature and he asked me if I saw the face in his picture of the sun and I know this is all one sentence, but that's the only way I can convey the energy coming from him as he talked to me. It's amazing the conversations one can have waiting in line at Fred Meyer's.

I went out to my car, and there was another young man feeding his jeep some kind of fuel enhancer in a bottle that I at first took for a soda can. He'd noticed my sticker for the Wake 'n Bakery in Glacier – and said he liked all my other stickers, too – and soon he was telling me about his *YouTube* snow reports and his horses and farm, and how he'd grown up in Michigan, but had lived in Marblemount for twenty years, and the difference between cross-country skiing in the topography of Michigan and cross-country skiing in the topography of the North Cascades and, again, I know that's a lot to put into one sentence, but that's the only way I can convey the energy I felt coming from THIS young man, too. It's amazing the conversations one can have in a parking lot at Fred Meyer's.

By the time I'd left Fred's I'd exchanged smiles, and made new friends, seen the good in the world, and seen the face of the sun.

July 19, 2024

A woman of about my age or a little younger was walking in front of me on the boardwalk and I suddenly had this vision of her as a little girl. It was like I was seeing her through the eyes of her mother.

I happened to run into her again at the coffee shop. I was impelled to tell her what I'd just experienced.

"Hi, this is maybe going to sound weird, but I just saw you walking in front of me as your mother saw you when you were a little girl, and she loved you very much." And then I started tearing up, and I think she started tearing up, too. There was something really profound in that moment.

When she left the coffee shop, she passed me and smiled a big smile and wished me a great day. And I wished her the same.

July 26, 2024

I met Ella and Kenzie, and Aidan and Finn, in Bellingham this morning. These young people give me hope for the world.

Ella and Kenzie are baristas at Fairhaven Coffee shop – and they are so fun! We talked for a bit about teaching – Ella's studying to be a music teacher, and Kenzie's studying to be a history teacher – and I shared my own background as a middle school social studies/English teacher and an alternative high school teacher. I loved their enthusiasm for teaching – I know their future students will be blessed to have them. They let me take their picture and gave me their names and then they asked my name and I said, "Karen, of course." We laughed together about the "Karen" thing for a moment, and then I said, "But that wasn't really your generation that came up with that, was it?" And they grinned and said no, that was the generation before them. Gen Zers are so cool.

Aidan and Finn were manning the Drizzles shop when I came in to buy a new bottle of Persian lime oil. Finn asked me if I'd like to try a sample of the Persian lime mixed with raspberry oil. I told him I would – and it was like candy! So of course I had to buy a bottle of the raspberry, too. Without mentioning any specific names in our conversation (we all knew who we were talking about), Finn and Aidan and I were able to carry on a dialogue about politics that gave me hope for the future of our country. They agreed to let me take their photo and gave me their names. Then Finn asked, "And what's your name?" I started laughing. "Get this!" I said, "I'm Karen!" Aidan and Finn got a good laugh out of this and Finn said, "You are the least Karen I know!"

(Yesterday when the barista at Wood's asked for a name for my mocha, I said "Karen" and he said, "Perfect!" – and I thanked him for that. He said he thinks the Karen meme is stupid and we gave each other high fives. I'm so enjoying the humor and attitude of our youngest adults.)

August 4, 2024

So here's where I was when I woke up in the middle of last night: I was feeling discouraged about the hate and lack of civility in the world; feeling disappointed in my own flaws and failures; feeling a deep sadness. Then I noticed Clara Cat wasn't in her usual place on the chair. I thought maybe somebody had let her outside and she hadn't gotten back in before we all went to bed. I looked for her on the back deck and on the front porch – but nada. And I got scared. We have coyotes and bobcats and eagles here.

I decided to pray, and I focused on getting my thoughts close to the God who is Love. I got all wrapped up in thinking about God as Love and feeling Her love for us. When I finally finished my prayer and looked up, I saw Clara lying on the top of the chair – all stretched out and casual – calmly looking at me.

And that one thing – seeing Clara healthy and content — put everything else in perspective and made the world look better. It was like a gentle pat on the back – a pat of reassurance from the God who is Love.

August 6, 2024

A perfect day! We did our annual hike up Table Mountain and met a cool young couple from Boston. James and Mariana were standing on top of Table Mountain. It looked to me like the perfect place for a proposal and I almost yelled out, "Say yes!" But I thought that might be rude if this was, like, their first date, so I kept my thoughts to myself. But on the way down we met up with them and learned that James HAD just proposed! And Mariana said yes! Then we learned that they'd just climbed Baker two days ago and wanted to get a better look at what they'd just climbed so had gone up Table Mountain for the view. We shared climbing stories then. (And…ahem… I MAY have mentioned my dad was in *Wikipedia* for climbing.) It's always so fun to meet new mountain people.

August 10, 2024

Grandbaby is cuddled up next to me in the crook of my arm. She's practicing different sounds with me – brrrr, thhpt, wudududuh – and watching my mouth as we make sounds together. Then she slides down off the couch and heads for the door. She looks back at me when she makes it to the door, and reaches for the handle. She's telling me she wants to go outside. When I get to the door, I look outside and see Andrew has come home from a day of filming. "Daddy's home!" I say to my granddaughter.

I pick her up and take her to the end of the driveway. She sees her daddy now, and her mommy standing beside him. She starts grinning. I set her down, and she race-toddles to Andrew – they're both laughing. The son gets down on his haunches to welcome her into his arms, and she settles inside his hug.

And I have a sudden memory of greeting my daddy the same way when he got home from work.

came

51

August 19, 2024

My niece, Claire, and her husband, Michael, and their little one, Yvonne, arrived two days ago from Montana to visit. Yvonne and Linh have finally met! Linh was born a year ago on July 19th Australian time, and Claire birthed her daughter half a day later on July 18th Montana time. And so, within half a day, my parents became great-grandparents of their first two great-grandchildren! I wish they had still been alive so that we could have celebrated with them in the person, but I felt them with us then, and I feel them with us now.

It's been so sweet to see Yvonne and Linh together – reaching out to touch each other's noses and give each other hugs. They splashed around in our toddler pool in the backyard yesterday – playing with water toys together - and I had a flashback of Claire and Andrew as toddlers, playing in my mom and dad's toddler pool 32 years ago. Cosmic!

Today we all went to Lake Padden and watched over the babies as they stepped into the water – cautiously at first, and then with more confidence. Later Christina, Claire, Kyla and I took the toddlers for a little hike along the shore of the lake. I hoisted Linh onto my shoulders for part of our walk. I could feel her bouncing around on my shoulders, grabbing onto my hair like it was a horse's main. When I peeked up at her, she was grinning. Her smile melts my heart.

August 31, 2024

Today was the fourth annual Bow Arts and Crafts and Thrift Sale. I had my books, photo cards and calendars set up under our blue canopy tent, and Andrew joined me with some of his hand-made art stickers.

Old friends stopped by to chat and buy our wares – Janice, Charlie, and Lynn came and gifted me with their hugs and smiles; and I was so happy to see my dear friend Rosemary appear in front of me! Rosemary told me the grant for her job had just ended and she wasn't sure what the future held. I told her I was going to give her one of my calendars – she could choose which one – and she needed to pick a day on the calendar and schedule it as a day she would find magic. Rosemary smiled a big smile – she liked the idea of scheduling a day for magic-finding – and chose one of my "Feathered Friends" calendars for herself.

the sale
It was a little quieter this year than previous years – I think because it was on a Labor Day weekend this year. But it was still fun to wander around the loop that makes up the Bow community – to chat with neighbors and friends; to buy home-made ice cream sandwiches from our new neighbor, Allison; to check out Paul's wood art and Brenda's quilts; to buy cookies from the neighbor boys; and to buy toys from Robert and Diana's "thrift shop" set up in their front yard.

Every year I look forward to seeing old friends and meeting new ones at our arts and crafts and thrift sale – actually selling things is really just an afterthought.

September 8, 2024

Scott and I and Andrew, Christina, and Linh are at Mount Rainier, celebrating my birthday month with some birthday hikes. I've met some new mountain friends while we've been here: Kaylin and Judd from Colfax; Luke from Colorado; David and Vicky from Vancouver, Canada; and Genesis and Ruby from Venezuela and their friends, Leydi and Silvana from Bolivia.

We met Kaylin and Judd on our hike up to Alta Vista yesterday – Kaylin is originally from South Carolina and the mountains are a new adventure for her. I don't think she'd ever hiked on a mountain trail before – but she was doing great! We took turns passing each other as we made our way up the nob that is Alta Vista, giving each other encouragement as we went. It was pretty cool to see her reach her first goal on a mountain hike, and I gave her well-deserved congratulations on getting to the top of Alta Vista.

We met Luke when he parked next to our car in the Paradise parking lot. I noted his mountain bike strapped onto the back of his car and told him it looked like he had all the essentials there. He laughed and said he had pretty much everything important with him in his car. Luke is traveling in the PNW having mountain adventures – he did some hiking on Hood a few days ago and hiked Rampart Ridge yesterday. He's planning on going up to Muir (the main base camp for the climb of Rainier) today and then heading up to Mount Baker next.

We met David and Vicki when we sat at the table next to them at the Inn and got into conversation. David and Vicky are staying at the Inn for a couple days and spending their days hiking the trails around Paradise.

I met Genesis and Ruby when I asked Genesis if she would take a picture of my family for me. Later I met Leydi and Silvana when I offered to take a picture of them together on the trail to Myrtle Falls. A few minutes later Genesis and Ruby joined them, and I found out they were all together – friends who met in an English class at Olympic College in Bremerton. Although the women were doing pretty well with their English, their first language was Spanish. Spanish happened to be one of Christina's majors in college – so Christina was able to converse with the women in their own tongue and translate what they were saying to the rest of us. I loved that she could do that for us.

Introducing Baby Linh to my old stomping grounds – the mountain where my parents had met seven decades ago – has meant a lot to me. It's been fun to watch Linh toddling along the trail, stopping to look up at the mountain every now and then.

Our time on the slopes of Rainier together – hiking old trails and meeting new friends - has been precious.

September 12, 2024

Christina's mum, Kim, arrived from Australia two days ago to spend time with us. It's been incredible to have her here, sharing in the joy of grandmotherhood with me. It fills my heart to have little Linh snuggled between us on the couch, smiling and happy to have BOTH her grandmas next to her.

We took Linh for a walk around the block yesterday – Kim and I taking turns pushing her in the stroller. Every now and then I'd sing Linh a song, and she'd bob her head in time to the music and lean left and right, and flex her feet up and down. Linh loves music.

Yesterday Xander and Kyla joined Kim, Christina, Andrew, Linh and I for a walk on the boardwalk in Bellingham. Linh loved walking between her grandmas – at one point Linh was holding Kim's hand and I was following behind, and Linh turned around and reached her free hand out for my hand – she wanted to make sure both her grandmas were with her.

What a gift to be in one of my favorite places, surrounded by people I love!

September 16, 2024

When Xander was in kindergarten I went to teaching half-time for the last part of the school year so that I could be off on the days Xander was off from kindergarten. One of the best days I've ever had was the day when Xander and I went to Washington Park in Anacortes on one of our days off and hiked down to Green Point together. We stayed there for a while, just relaxing, and then he turned to me and asked, "Isn't this nice, Mommy?" I asked him what was nice, and he said, "Just sitting here in the sunshine with you." And that. Right there. That sweet memory has stayed with me for twenty-five years.

I went back to Washington Park today and walked down to Green Point again. I ran into a little family – father, mother, baby, grandma – and enjoyed watching them spend time together, enjoying each other, and I thought of the day I spent there in the sunshine with Xander.

I had the opportunity to talk to the family for a bit. I learned that the little one, Fiona, was just a few months younger than my granddaughter. She was sitting on her daddy's shoulders – flapping her arms up and down like my granddaughter does when she's on my shoulders or her Grampa Scott's. Then Fiona turned and pointed to me – just as my granddaughter does – and I pointed back. Fiona started grinning, enjoying our game.

I learned this was the first time Fiona's grandmother had been able to see her and spend time with her, and she was leaving to go back to her home in Pakistan on Wednesday. My grandma's heart went out to her. I know this feeling.

I thought at first that there were colorful shreds from popped party balloons strewn on the grass at Green Point. Then I realized the colorful shreds were actually rose petals. Rose petals seemed fitting for the day.

September 17, 2024

I heard a train coming as I walked on the boardwalk and tried to get behind the knoll before it showed up – hoping the hill would buffer some of the noise. I didn't make it to the knoll, and I'm glad about that because, instead of the monster freight train I was expecting, a fleet-wheeled passenger train appeared. I grinned and started waving and the engineer waved back! Then the conductor who was standing between the cars gave me a wave, and then a passenger waved through the window! And another passenger waved! Four people! That's a new record for me!

I stopped by Village Books to use my reward points for the latest Richard Osman book (which just came out today) – and when I went to pay I realized I had nabbed a signed copy!

And then, when I was almost back to my car, I saw one of my former eighth graders, Donato, delivering flowers (his mom owns three flower shops!) to the Fairhaven florist. It was so awesome to see Donato again!

It's only 10:30 and look at all the cool things that have already happened!

September 18, 2024

I had a free coffee waiting for me at Beaver Tales coffee shop in La Conner, and thought that might be a nice way to start my day.

As I was driving into La Conner I passed a pumpkin display at the roundabout that completely dazzled me! I picked up my free pumpkin spice latte and then made my way to the Hedlin's Family Farm stand. Jules, the owner, was there, working on the pumpkin display. I told her I was blown away by what she'd created there. I asked her if all these pumpkins were grown on her farm, and she said they were. Her favorite, she said, were the variety called "Troll." I could see why – Trolls are like something out of a fairy tale – all chunky and mottled and sort of other-worldly looking. I had to get one of those. I also got a teeny tiny little pumpkin for Linh, and a bouquet of cheery sunflowers and zinnias. It was magic there.

September 22, 2024

Today, Kim, Christina, and Linh joined me for a walk through La Conner. We stopped at the bookstore and the bookstore lady read a children's book to Linh. We stopped at the ice cream stand and I took a picture of Kim, Christina, and Linh sticking their faces through an ice cream photo cut out board – Linh was so cute with her little face sticking through the hole at the bottom! We walked down the La Conner boardwalk, looking at boats and birds and meeting people and their pups. And after we'd toured the town, we went to the Hedlin's Farm to look at the pumpkin and autumn flower displays.

It was such a fun day!

I've so enjoyed having Kim here with us. I'm going to miss her when she leaves. We're family.

September 23, 2024

I heard the telltale thump on the dining room window and ran around the house to see if I could help. The robin was lying on the ground, not moving, but I could see he was still breathing. I gently scooped him into my hands and began to talk to him: "God is your Life. You are the perfect, whole, complete expression of Love. You live in the realm of Good – you are never outside of God's governance – never separated from Love." And I softly sang one of my favorite hymns to him: "Everlasting arms of Love are beneath, around, above."

The robin watched me and listened to me and seemed to be comfortable in my hands. He didn't seem at all scared of me.

When I first picked him up his beak was open, and I wondered if his beak was injured in some way. I saw blood in my palm and realized he had a wound on his breast. I continued to affirm to myself and to the little robin that he was safe and whole and embraced in Love, and slowly his beak closed.

I brought him up to the deck and put him in a flower box on the railing. I kept stroking his back, and talking to him, and he stayed there, listening. Then I asked, "Are you ready to fly now?" And he lifted up his wings – just like that! – and flew over to the fencing around the blueberry patch.

I whooped to him from the deck: "Have a wonderful day, little one!"

I knew I was walking on holy ground.

September 26, 2024

Between Two Grandma-Nanas
I walk a pace behind
as she holds Nana Kim's hand
and she reaches back
for my hand, too -
what is better than walking
between TWO grandma-nanas?
I sit on the couch, reading,
and little one toddles in,
looks at me, and points
to the other part of the house -
she wants me to join her
and Nana Kim in the family room.
Nana Kim and I sit in chairs kitty-corner
and bounce our grandbaby
back and forth between us
and she giggles and laughs.
What could be better than bouncing
between TWO grandma-nanas?
She grabs my hand and leads me
to the door. She wants to go outside.
I call to Nana Kim that our grandbaby
wants to go for a walk and invite her
to join us. Then I bring the stroller
off the porch and strap Grandbaby in.
She looks up to see Grandma Kim
has joined us and her face
opens wide into a grin.
What could be better than being
between TWO grandma-nanas?!

September 30, 2024

Grandbaby, son and daughter-in-law left yesterday to make their home in California. It felt like all the energy and life had been sucked out of our house when they left. My instincts told me it was time to head for the mountains - my healing place.

My original destination was Artist Point, but the road was closed past Church Mountain, so I turned off into a parking spot near the north fork of the Nooksack River and sauntered along a trail I'd never sauntered before - the Horseshoe Bend trail. It was just exactly what I needed. Along the way I met other folks who had planned to go to Artist Point today, but found themselves on the Horseshoe Bend trail with me - Kelsie was one of these, and she let me snap a picture of her sweet pup, Ender. Later I ran into Bob and Cecelia from Maryland and had a delightful chat with them about mountaineering and living in different parts of the country and the way cool behemoth van they were traveling around in.

When I'd parked in the parking lot for the trailhead, I'd been the third car there. By the time I left I counted 21 vehicles - including the way cool behemoth van that must have transported my new friends there.

October 5, 2024

Scotty and I went up to Mount Rainier yesterday to walk around in the autumn colors. Last week the weather forecast predicted sunshine up there, but that changed. It was pretty wet, but it was still beautiful. I thought my camera was doing some sort of weird automatic "vignette" with my photos (fading my photos out at the corners), but then I realized my lens filter was actually all fogged-up on the rim.

Highlights: On the drive up to Paradise from Longmire, I glanced over at a parking lot by the Nisqually Glacier (or where the glacier USED to be), and saw a familiar van – I was pretty sure this was the same behemoth van I'd seen at Mount Baker last week, and I was pretty sure it belonged to my new friends, Cecelia and Bob. Whoah. So I messaged them, and learned that they were at Rainier, too! Cosmic!

We went into the Paradise gift shop at the Visitor Center and chatted with the pair of salesclerks behind the counter. I told them I'd worked in the old Visitor Center almost 50 years ago – back when the Visitor Center looked like an alien spacecraft. They laughed and said the old Visitor Center had flown back to the Mother Ship.

I found one of Dad's books in the giftshop. It's always fun to come upon his books or maps in tourist hangouts. It helps me feel he's still here with us.

At Myrtle Falls, we came upon a couple of National Park employees getting the trails ready for winter. I thanked them for their service and we chatted for a bit about climbing. Noah and Carter were pretty fun and graciously agreed to let me snap a photo.

Then, as we were coming back from the Falls, a little family of sooty grouse (I mistook them for ptarmigans at first) crossed our path (literally) and we snapped some quick pics.

We visited the Ashford Creek Pottery shop on the way up to Rainier yesterday to visit its proprietor, our old friend Rick Johnson, and to take pictures of the artwork of Dad's that Rick has hanging on the walls. I also got Rick to pose with art by Todd Horton (who, coincidentally, lives in the same Skagit Valley community as us), and to pose with one of Dad's books.

(I think the painting that most tickled me yesterday was one Dad had painted depicting mountains of Alaska – and in which he'd whimsically added the Matterhorn in the background. I was looking at the painting, and then thought, "Whoah. That's the Matterhorn there. What's THAT doing there?" It put a grin on my face. Oh, Dad. Hahhahhahahar!)

October 6, 2024

Just as I was starting my boardwalk walk today, I passed a pair of friends, Dupree and Bella, sitting next to a stroller. Ever since I became a grandma 14 months ago, I am drawn to strollers like a magnet to a fridge door. So I had to ask for a peek at Bella's baby, and then I chatted with the two friends for a while. I learned that Dupree and Bella had met at the Northwest Indian College, and I shared that a couple of my former students had attended there, too. Bella let me get a peek at her little one – he was so cute! And then the two friends let me snap their picture.

I went on down to Boulevard Park and took some photos of the autumn leaves.

On the way back I passed, again, a pair of friends, Dan and Toby, and I just had to stop and ask Dan about the shirt he was wearing. "I've passed you guys a couple of times now and I just have to ask – what is that?" I asked, pointing at the outlined illustration on Dan's shirt. Dan smiled and told me it was an otter – and once he told me what it was, it was like "duh" – of course, that's an otter. I told Toby and Dan that otters are one of my favorite animals and shared with them the time I'd seen six or seven otters playing around on the old dock that used to be at the end of Boulevard Park. They thought that was pretty cool. They graciously agreed to let me take their picture.

When I got to Taylor Dock, I saw three friends leaning against the railing – two of them were wet, and one was dry. "Did you go in the water?" I asked Joel, and he laughed and said yes. He said that he works a lot in Alaska, though, so this water doesn't really feel that cold to him. Then I pointed to Angel – "You're dry!" I said, and he smiled and said he hadn't wanted to go in – which made perfect sense to me – that water has GOT to be cold. A couple more friends joined the original three and they all posed for me at the railing so's I could get their photo.

As I was coming up the ramp I heard someone calling my name and looked over to see my friend Rosemary sitting on a bench on the ramp. Okay, this was kind of cosmic because the first place I remember meeting Rosemary was on that ramp six years ago. Rosemary said she'd really been hoping she'd run into me today, but didn't think it likely because she knows I usually come in the morning. But I'd felt led to go up there this afternoon, and now I know why. Rosemary was glowing – that's the only word that describes it – her face was all lit up with joy. She shared then that she'd decided to stay in the Pacific Northwest rather than return to the east coast. She realized this was her home now – and once she'd come to that realization she felt at peace. How wonderful! I started tearing up – feeling my friend's peace with Life.

On the way home along Chuckanut Drive I pulled over to enjoy the sunset over the water. A car with a California license plate pulled up in front of me and four young people bounced out of it to enjoy the sunset with me. It was nice to be able to share the magic with them.

I'm guessing (hoping?) I'm not the only one who does this: I'll find myself drawn to people in supermarkets and on my walks - youngsters and midsters and oldsters, of every shade and color, costume and culture and gender - and I'll throw out a hope to the Cosmos that I'll have the chance to exchange joy and laughter with these people before we pass each other and head off on our separate journeys through life. And often - usually, in fact - the Cosmos responds to my hopes. Today I had the chance to experience this again.

I stopped at Fred Meyer's for some quick shopping. As I was looping through the aisles I passed a tall Black man of about my age and I felt kindness emanating from him. I sent out a hope to the Cosmos that the opportunity would come for me to talk with him. I wasn't going to push this - it had to be organic and natural, and part of the deal with the Cosmos is that I have to accept when the connection doesn't happen and let it go.

I saw the man heading for the checkout line, and thought that this time I'd have to let it go.

I ran into a neighbor - that was fun! And there was a little traffic jam in the aisle on the way out - "You first," I said, smiling at a man in a way cool t-shirt with a rainbow and a comma 'la on it - "What a great shirt!" I told him, and he laughed and thanked me.

I was in the threshold area of the store now and looked over and there he was - the man I'd passed earlier in the store! I glanced down and saw he was holding a UW shopping bag, and I asked him if he was a UW alum. He smiled and said he was. I told him I'd graduated from WSU, but my dad had gone to UW, and we'd always had fun during the Apple Cup. He grinned and acknowledged that the Cougs had done a good job of it this year. "Yeah, I felt pretty good about that," I told him, and he laughed and said, "I bet you did." I asked him how he felt about the UW leaving the Pac-12, and he said he didn't really like that. I told him I didn't think my dad would have liked that, either. Dad and I had enjoyed our friendly school rivalry. My new friend smiled and nodded.

It was time to go on our separate journeys now. My new friend smiled and wished me a good day and I wished him the same.

October 9, 2024

Last week Xander and I planned a trip up to Mount Baker for today. But this morning when I woke up and checked the weather it looked like it was pretty miserable up there. Xander and I decided to call the trip off.

A couple hours later, though, when I checked the weather again, it looked like there might actually be some sunshine at Baker. So I texted Xander and told him about the change in the weather forecast, and asked him if he'd like to give it a try. Then I opened my thoughts up to the Cosmos and put the day in Her hands. I decided I'd be happy with however the day evolved for me.

Pretty soon Xander texted back and said he still wanted to go up there. Within the hour I'd picked him up and we were on the road.

When we arrived we found the weather was glorious! We stopped at Picture Lake to take some quick pictures of the gold and copper of the autumn fauna, and Mount Shuksan rising up in the background (we got there at the just right time – not long after we left, the clouds moved in and blanketed Shuksan). We did a quick little hike on the nature trail at Heather Meadows. Then we parked in the highest parking lot and hiked up to the top of Artist Point.

On the way up we came upon a bride and groom, Sarah and Etienne, in full wedding regalia, and they cheerfully agreed to let me snap a quick photo. Later I asked a couple from Canada if they'd like me to take a picture of them together with their camera and they thanked me and said yes. On the way down we ran into them again, and this time I asked Kathy if I could take a picture of her with her sweet pup, Coriander.

It was such a lovely day with Xander. He lets me lead and follows at my pace - even though I know he could go much faster if he wanted – and he stops with me now and then to just breathe in the alpine air and take in the view. I can also feel him watching out for

me in the same way I watched out for him when he was a child –
"Careful there!" he'll say with a laugh, as I make my way through
a steep section of trail. Xander knows how to enjoy the mountains,
and he knows how to make me smile.

As we were coming down from Artist Point, I had a flashback to
that moment when Xander turned to me at Green Point in
Washington Park and asked, "Isn't this nice, Mommy?"

Yes. Yes, Xander, it is.

October 18, 2024

I had this moment yesterday – sitting in the Colophon Cafe in Bellingham – that was perfect. I felt my whole body just relax, and this big sigh came out of me. My eyes closed and I listened to the folksy music playing in the background, and the conversations and laughter of the diners around me, and – for just a glimmer of a moment – I was sitting in heaven. I'm trying to find the words to describe it, and I'm trying to find the words to help me get back there, but I don't think there are the just right words that fit that experience. I think that moment was beyond words. But here are the words that come closest: For a brief moment I felt no time, no hurry, no schedule, no expectations, no past, no future, and nothing crowding in on me. I felt joy, peace, love. I felt space. I felt in the present. I felt safe.

There were three people sitting at the table across from me – maybe my age or a little younger. And I felt this positive energy coming from them. (If I were more educated about this stuff, I might say I felt "positive auras" surrounding them – but I don't know enough about auras to use that word and really know what I'm talking about.) I think they were having a business meeting of some sort. I couldn't pick up on all that they were saying, but these snippets reached me:

Woman with curly silver hair in a high ponytail: People tell me they sometimes have to take a break from me because of my energy. (Laughing.) And I understand that, but I tell them if they think it's hard being AROUND me, can they imagine what it's like to actually BE me? Sometimes *I* need a break from me!

A little later…

Ponytailed woman: It seems as we get older we go one of two directions – either we become more crotchety, more crabby, more…

71

Woman with dark, shoulder-length hair: (Laughing.) We become more of what we already are.

The iron-haired man sitting next to the dark-haired woman – her husband maybe? – winced at this and started laughing, and I found myself laughing with him.

It got me to thinking. What direction am "I" headed? What am I becoming more of?

And how can I bring more of these perfect moments into my life?

October 21, 2024

I've been feeling a little off-kilter lately – maybe feeling the tension of the political season and the stress of the folks around me. I love autumn, but there are certain aspects of October in our country that can be challenging for those of us who live here.

Then I got a message from my friend, Emmy, daughter-in-law of the late great Pete Schoening (who saved my dad's life on K2), asking if I was available to meet at the Shambala Bakery in Mount Vernon today – and I was! And we did! And it was so wonderful to chat with Emmy again – she's one of those people I feel an instant kinship with – funny and kind and honest. We always laugh when we get together.

As we were eating our brunch, a customer in a baseball cap and a Grateful Dead shirt came through the door. There was something whacky with the door – we'd noticed this when we came in – and when the customer noticed it he started examining the hinges and the frame. Emmy and I realized he was going to try to fix it.

How cool is that?

Pretty soon the customer had borrowed tools from the server-cashier-cook, and retrieved some tools from his truck, and was working on the door.

I asked Justin, the customer-handyman, and Heidi, the server-cook, if I could take their picture, and they graciously agreed. Then Heidi went back to work, Emmy and I finished our brunch, and Justin finished fixing the door. I observed to Justin that he'd done a really nice thing there. He said that he couldn't just let that door stay broken. He wanted to make it good for Shambala.

Laughing with Emmy, and watching the man in the Grateful Dead shirt fix the door, helped settle me this morning. There are good people in this world.

73

October 24, 2024

Little jewels from the last couple of days:

I pull into the Fred Meyer parking lot and park off to the side near the gardening center. As I'm getting my shopping bag and backpack-purse out of my car, a tall man – probably a little younger than me, with the build of a retired quarterback – returns to his truck. His truck is parked near my car. He is wearing a red hat and I'm pretty sure I know what it says on it.

I feel suddenly impelled to exchange a greeting with him, but I let the Cosmos decide what's going to happen here, and finish getting out my stuff. When I go to get a shopping cart in the little cart corral, he's pushing in a small cart. His red hat does, indeed, say what I thought it would say.

"It's getting colder!" I observe – weather is always a good place to start, right? He smiles and agrees with me. I notice him glance at my little Fiesta hatchback and I'm sure he's taking in the bumper stickers there: "GOD BLESS THE WHOLE WORLD. NO EXCEPTIONS." "MAKE AMERICA GREEN AGAIN." And whatnot. He glances back at me and smiles. I'm pretty sure he knows we're from different tribes.

"Do you need a cart?" he asks, offering me the one he just put back, and I smile back at him and thank him, and take the cart from him into the supermarket. I'm still smiling as I enter the store. There is kindness in every tribe.

I pick up the items I need to pick up and check out, then head to the Starbucks counter. Gabriel, the barista – tall, Black, with a longish goatee dyed flamingo-pink – steps up to take my order. I love this guy. He never fails to make me smile. He asks what I'd like and I tell him this will be my first coffee in a month. He gasps. "Honey!" he exclaims in horror, "We need to fix that for you!" While he's making my pumpkin spice latte he regales me with tales of his dogs and his husband and his grocery-shopping experiences. By the time he hands me my latte I have had a whole day's worth of laugh-out-louds. He is like a one-man comedy show. As I leave, I tell a couple of the workers who are sitting at the exit that "I love that guy!" And they nod their heads and laugh. They get it.

I go to the Target parking lot to take pictures of the autumnal trees and then go into the store to explore what they've got in there. As I'm browsing, I wander down the coffee aisle and see there are a lot of coffee options for Keurig owners, but we are not Keurig owners – so that's not going to work. There are also, though, bags of ground coffee, and I think, "Oh! I should get one of those French presses and press my own coffee!" So I ask a man stocking shelves if he knows where I might find French presses. He's really helpful – tells me his wife uses a French press every morning to make her own coffee – and then clicks into his Target device and tells me what aisle I can find French presses in.

I proudly bring my French press home…

The next morning I'm back in Target to return the French press. I tell the customer service lady what happened: "I came home and showed my husband the French press and he said, 'Karen. We already have two of those.'" The customer service woman starts cracking up and, as she's efficiently taking care of my return for me, suggests maybe I should buy one for every day of the week. I love people who make me laugh.

On the way home I decide to turn onto Allen West Road just to see what magic I can find there. And there's that amazing pumpkin display I remember seeing last October! Darla, the owner of Eagle View Farms, comes out to greet me, a big smile on her face.

"Karen!" she calls – she remembers my name!

It's so good to see Darla again. It's our annual reunion, I guess. We talk about her son, Adam, who was in my eighth-grade class a couple decades ago – a very cool person – and laugh and chat and laugh some more. She's covered in mud. She says she's been cleaning out the gutters while her husband went shopping. I say, dreamily, "Sounds like a Hallmark movie," and she laughs out loud.

I snap some pictures of her display, and then buy a big yellow pumpkin from her. I ask her how much – there are no signs indicating the price – and she says, "Seven dollars."

"How much REALLY?" I ask. And she insists it's seven dollars. Right. So I write her a check for ten, she calls me a stinker, and I ask her how much it really is. She admits it's ten dollars.

We hug one more time – mud and all – and I drive home with a big yellow pumpkin and my heart full of humanity's goodness.

October 25, 2024

I want to share a healing I had this week.

Monday night I discovered that there had been a weird billing error – well, TWO weird billing errors, actually – one from my insurance company and another one from the optometrist's office. The errors had resulted in the wrong person getting charged for one of my visits to the optometrist – a bill that should have been covered by my insurance, in the first place. When I first learned of the snafu(s), I was pretty stressed, and a little angry on behalf of the innocent family member who'd erroneously been listed as the "guarantor" for my bill.

I couldn't get to sleep and eventually came downstairs to pray about this situation. Soon I was filled with this feeling of joy and well-being, and it felt like Love was laughing with me about the absurdity of it all, and reassuring me that all was well.

The next morning I woke up early, and at exactly 8:00 am I called the insurance office. A man named Loren answered the phone. I asked him if he had time to hear a really weird story, and he said he did, so I began to lay out the problem I was having with this bill. He listened and every now and then interjected some comment or question. He was very patient with me as I pulled out all the cards from my wallet, trying to find the one with my ID number on it, and when I thanked him for his patience, I could hear the smile in his voice as he told me it was okay. At one point I apologized for being so chatty when I knew he must be tapping away on his keyboard and trying to figure out what the problem was – and he laughed and said he was fine – he was good at multi-tasking. He was kind and patient and had a sense of humor, and in a short time he'd pinpointed the problem and assured me that I didn't need to worry about this anymore – the insurance company would take care of the bill for me.

I asked, "So I didn't do anything wrong?" his voice smiled again, and he reassured me that I'd done everything right. I told him I wanted to give him a good rating, He thanked me for that and said he would try to send me through to his manager. I started laughing. "Yes, I am Karen and I want to talk to your manager." He started laughing then, too.

At 8:30 on the dot I called the optometrist's office, and a woman named Savannah picked up. When she looked at my account she said a note had already been made there by the insurance company and that I didn't need to worry about this bill anymore. "I don't need to worry about this? It's taken care of?" I asked. And she said yup, I could just throw this bill away. Then I asked her if I could have something in writing about this – I told her I am Karen AND a Virgo AND a boomer – basically, "I'm the trifecta of annoying" – and she started laughing and said she'd send me an email. Within minutes after we'd ended our phone call she had sent an email telling me that the bill was being sent back to the insurance company for payment and I didn't need to worry about it.

It was such a lovely untangling. There was so much joy and humor and kindness involved in the whole experience. I'm really grateful for this opportunity to prove Love's power.

October 30, 2024

Yesterday I thought I'd make my monthly trip to La Conner to pay my Astound bill and look for snow geese and whatever other magic I could find along the way.

I wound through the lowlands near my home in Bow and ended up on Farm-to-Market Road, where I spotted snow geese taking off and landing on a snow geese airstrip in a field somewhere to the east. I turned onto D'arcy and headed east, keeping an eye out for snow geese, but couldn't spot them anywhere. I headed north on Edison-Bayview, headed east on Sunset, south on Thomas, saw a couple of trumpeter swans overhead and followed them for a while, and somehow ended up on Pulver. I decided to take Pulver across Highway 20 and work myself to La Conner from there.

I stopped off at Christianson's Nursery on the way, knowing I would find some autumn magic there. The folks at Christianson's were starting to set up for Christmas, but I was still able to find the autumn wonders I was looking for – shiny, round pumpkins and trees aglow in copper and gold leaves.

As I continued along Best Road to the turn to La Conner, I came upon a raucous murmuration of snow geese moving in waves across a field off Calhoun Road. Oh, the joy of hearing them up-close again! I stayed with them for a while, snapping photos and getting videos, and letting their squawks and honks clean out the stored-up sounds of modern machinery that have built up in my soul since they've been gone.

When I got to Astound, both Jeri and Jolyne were there, and in fine form. Jolyne and I talked politics for a bit - Jolyne leans right and I lean left, and I always enjoy talking with her about political issues and listening to her articulate and reasoned take on things. She always grins when I come into the office - she knows what's coming.

I hadn't eaten breakfast, yet, and decided to walk to the Calico Cupboard to get myself some Pesto Focaccia Scramble (scrambled eggs with pesto and focaccia mixed in - yum!). The hostess-server at Calico Cupboard recognized me when I walked in and said it was good to see me again. It was good to see her again, too. She is one of the good people woven into the fabric of my community of good people.

After I paid for breakfast, I stopped off at the Calico Cupboard bakery to buy one of their famous cinnamon rolls and get myself a peanut butter chocolate thing, too. The cashier was a hoot - friendly and funny - one of those people with the timing and wit of a natural comedian. At one point she said she was sorry (I still don't know what she was apologizing for). "Yeah, you SHOULD be," I said. She started laughing. "And just for that I'm going to have to give you a big tip. For the free entertainment," I told her.

A week or so ago I'd sent off an autumn letter to one of my former teaching colleagues at West View (our local dual-language school), but it had come back to me stamped with "NOT AT THIS ADDRESS." So I figured I'd just stop by West View and hand it to my friend in person. I hadn't seen Teresa in years and was looking forward to seeing her face again.

It was cool to be at West View again - the halls were filled with smiles and the sounds of children's laughter as they lined up to go to the cafeteria. After I'd checked in at the office, Raven, one of the office assistants, offered to take me to Teresa's kindergarten class. When Teresa looked up and saw me, she came over to give me a big hug. A little girl followed Teresa over to me, leaned against me, and put her little hand in mine. She looked up at me with big brown eyes and told me her name was Estafania, and then skipped off to play with her friends. That little hand in mine was one of the highlights of my whole day.

Home again - my heart full of laughter and snow geese honks and kindergarten sweetness - I settled into my favorite chair to process photos and the magic of the day.

November 2, 2024

Life gave me an incredible gift today.

A month or so ago an old student of mine from Emerson High School texted me to see if we could meet for coffee. I was surprised, but not, to hear from Hector.

I'd been thinking of him – remembering the time we'd been taking turns reading out loud from an astronomy book, and he'd read a passage that said something like: "The stars you see in the night sky are bringing you a story from thousands of years ago." His head had popped up and his eyebrows had come together in a puzzled frown. "What's that supposed to mean?" he'd asked.

I told him that the light we see from the stars took thousands of years to reach us – so we're not seeing the light from the stars as they are right now – we're seeing the light from the stars as they were thousands of years ago.

His eyebrows lifted then and his eyes got huge. "WHOAH. That's CRAZY!" he'd exclaimed. And then he'd started talking about how cool it would be to be an astronaut.

I hadn't seen Hector for several years and was wondering how he was doing – hoping all was well with him – so when he'd texted out of the blue, it felt like a cosmic coincidence to me.

We arranged to meet today at Whidbey Coffee in Burlington. And oh! It was so good to see Hector again! He is a remarkable young man.

We hugged and I bought us coffees (he told me I didn't need to buy his coffee for him, but I insisted) and we settled into a couple of comfortable chairs near the window. And for the next two hours we talked and laughed and got caught up. Hector's life has changed a lot since I last saw him. He felt the need to make a new start for himself and moved to Seattle to work with his brother in carpentry.

He loves his work as a carpenter – he showed me the houses he'd helped build – he said he did everything in building the houses except the drywalling. He's excited about all he's learning on his job. He showed me photos and videos from his backpacking trips – he said he found a group of friends in Seattle who introduced him to hiking and rock-climbing – and he's totally hooked on outdoors adventures now. Last summer, he told me, he hiked 25 miles in one day in the Enchantments. He showed me his photos from the trip – and his photos showed his talent for capturing the beauty around him.

Then Hector told me that he's gotten big into jujitsu – trains for competitions – and during the course of his training he discovered one of his favorite sparring partners was a pastor at a church in Seattle. In connecting with this pastor he found a church community and found God. He was so excited about all he's learning about God's love, and so eager to share what he's learned.

He said one of his favorite passages in the Bible is the one about building your house on sand. When we'd talked about Hector's carpentry, we'd talked about the importance of a house being "plumb" – if the first floor is plumb, square, and level then the floors above the first floor will be, too. So the parable of the house built on the sand means something to Hector, the carpenter. He said if you build a house on the sand you can keep adding on to it – floor after floor – more and more – and it can be a 10-story house, but if that first floor is built on sand then it's all going to come down in a windstorm. You need to build your foundation on the rock, he said – on God.

I told him it seemed that God had been leading him to this spiritual place, and he smiled and nodded and agreed. He asked me, then, about my own experience with God – and, for the first time –

because he's no longer my student – I felt free to share my own spiritual journey with him.

I asked Hector what had led him to text me. He thought for a moment and then said that he'd had struggles in high school – he hadn't really liked school until he came to me as a contract-based student, working with me one-on-one. He said he felt heard when he was with me. He felt safe. He felt loved.

I started tearing up then. The Cosmos knew what I needed today – and the Cosmos sent me Hector.

November 6, 2024

Yesterday - Election Day - I woke at two in the morning feeling like I was riding on a collective wave of joy – like I was part of a cosmic celebration. I hadn't had that feeling before an election since… well, I don't think I've ever had that feeling before an election, so I took this feeling as a good sign – as a sign that everything was going to go as I hoped it would.

And when things didn't go as I hoped, I found myself in a crisis, wondering if everything I believe about the power of Love and Truth is a lie. Wondering if there really is a God.

What was kind of odd, though, was that – even as I was having these dark thoughts – I could feel Love with me, loving me. But I turned away from that sense of Love-with-me and tossed and turned for a while before I finally got to sleep.

Here's what happened today:

– Xander called to see how I was doing and just hearing his voice through the line – and hearing Kyla's laughter in the background – lifted me up.

– I decided to go for a hike at Lake Padden. On the way I pulled over, and put my emergency lights on, to take a picture of a reflection on Lake Samish. Before I even got out of the car, another car did a u-turn and the driver – a twenty-something with piercings on her face, and a kind smile – pulled in behind me to check on me and make sure I was alright. I was so grateful for her kindness in stopping to check on me! I felt myself lifted up a bit more.

– As I sat at a picnic table at Lake Padden, a little dog named Lock trotted over to me for a pet on his back. He sat with me for several minutes as I petted him, every now and then looking up at me with a look of pure love on his face. It was like having my own emotional support dog there, comforting me with his sweetness.

– I passed a woman named April, with her dog, Aspen. Like Lock, Aspen approached me for a scratch behind the ears. And when April and I got to talking we realized we were both processing the same election shock. Pretty soon we were joined by Judy, who also was dealing with election trauma. We gave each other a group hug, and then Judy let us know that there was a young woman sitting up at the picnic table who was struggling. So April and I (and Aspen) went to join the woman at the picnic table. She was wearing a gay pride rainbow hat, and she was soon joined by two friends who let us know they were from the LGBTQ community. The woman in the rainbow hat and her friends were all feeling scared and abandoned by their country. April and I let them know that they aren't alone – that we're standing together with them.

– When I got home I clicked into *Facebook* and found my friend, Jay Bowen, had posted a post about a vigil being held at the Burlington Lutheran Church. So I zipped my jacket back on and headed for the church.

I hadn't really cried, yet, but as soon as I entered the church I felt tears welling up in my eyes, and by the time I'd seated myself on a pew I was quietly sobbing and shaking – I hadn't know that was in me until then. A woman in the pew ahead of me turned around and it was Becky! – a parent of one of my former eighth graders. Becky went up to the first pew and grabbed a box of tissues for me and then came back and gave me a hug. Not long after I saw Becky, I recognized another friend, Kaci, seated in the second row. I approached Kaci and touched her arm, and when she turned around and saw me, her eyes opened wide and she reached out for a hug. We cried healing tears together for a couple of minutes, before I returned to my pew.

The speakers in the Lutheran church spoke of allowing people to mourn in their own way; spoke of the courage and endurance that have overcome tribulation in the past; spoke of the importance of community and family; spoke of the importance of appreciating every breath and moment; spoke of not letting anyone take our smiles and humor; and spoke of a loving God whose intent isn't to bring us doom, but to bring healing to us and through us.

It was comforting to be with other people today who were dealing with the same things I'm dealing with.

And now, sitting here, I realize the message the Cosmos has been sending me all day: "You are not alone. The world is full of people (and pups) who care. You are loved." And maybe that's all the reason I need to celebrate with the Cosmos. Maybe the wave of joy I felt early in the morning on election day had nothing to do with the election, and everything to do with divine Love. Love is not dependent on human circumstances, and we can never be separated from Her.

November 15, 2024

Xander and Kyla have been looking at houses to buy. We'd looked at a couple of houses with them in the Sudden Valley neighborhood, and they were interested in offering on one, but, in the end, felt it just wasn't the right place for them. A few days after they made that decision an atmospheric bomb cyclone hit the Pacific Northwest, and Sudden Valley – which is mostly in a forest - was hit particularly hard. Huge trees were blown onto houses, cars and roads, and there was a power outage that lasted several days. We all were grateful that Xander and Kyla hadn't made an offer on that house.

Yesterday Kyla texted me that she'd made an appointment to look at a house in the little town of Sedro-Woolley today, and she wanted to know if I'd like to look at it with her. I clicked on the photo she sent me of the house and immediately started grinning. This! This was their house! I just knew it! It was painted forest green with clean white trim and a welcoming porch and I'm pretty sure that house was smiling at me.

Kyla picked me up and we drove to Sedro-Woolley together. Kyla has roots in Sedro-Woolley – she'd graduated from Sedro-Woolley High School. And, when Xander and Andrew were youngsters, we'd lived in Sedro-Woolley, too. So there was this feeling of "going home" when we drove through the town.

The house was just as welcoming in person as it had been in the picture. And when we looked at the house across the street we saw it had a rainbow flag hanging from its porch. We took this as a good sign.

I think as soon as we stepped through the door Kyla knew this was her house. We took a tour of the inside and outside, and, before we even drove away, Kyla had called Xander and asked him to put in an offer on the home.

Okay, before I go further into our day, I think I need to do a quick flashback here: A few weeks ago Kyla introduced me to the *Twilight* movies. I'd never been interested in them, but Kyla told me they were some of the funniest movies she'd ever seen – wonderfully and extravagantly cheesy. These were the movies that Kyla had watched with her friends when she was in middle school and high school – at an age when everything seems so big and dramatic - when you have your first crush and you think you will "never love like that again."

Kyla had already introduced me to two of my all-time favorite movies – *Eurovision* and *Hunt for the Wilderpeople* – so I trusted her with this. And, once again, Kyla was right – *Twilight* was fantastically, hilariously cheesy, but there was also a kind of nostalgic tenderness to it. As a former middle school teacher, my heart went out to these characters. I wanted to tell them that what seemed so big and catastrophic to them right now was going to take on a whole different perspective in a decade or two. I mean. Assuming there aren't actually vampires amongst us.

So after we looked at the house that might soon become Xander and Kyla's home, we went back to my home, popped some popcorn, and watched the next installment in the *Twilight* series. We laughed and, simultaneously, wanted to give these poor angst-ridden young people hugs. It was weirdly cathartic. Maybe the *Twilight* movies help ME put things in perspective, too.

November 17, 2024

King tide, high water, drenching rain - the boardwalk was fantastic this morning!

Another boardwalk walker had stopped to take photos of the high water and I stopped to chat with her. Her face lit up when she saw me and she asked me my name. I told her "Karen" and she said she'd been enjoying my posts in "The Seeing Bellingham" group on *Facebook*. How cool! I asked her name then, and she told me she was Robin - and I told her I recognized her name, too! We've been *Facebook* friends since July! It was fun to finally meet Robin in the person.

A little farther down the trail another walker stopped to enjoy the rain and high water with me. "Isn't it FANTASTIC?!" I asked him.

"Yes, it is the big tide," he said with a brilliant smile and an accent I think might have been from India. And, as I turned to continue on my walk, he said, "Have a good day!" I turned back and smiled and wished him the same.

A little girl and her mom were walking under an umbrella in front of me. There was something about the two of them under that umbrella that charmed me. When I got to them, I asked if I could take a picture of them from the back (so the little girl's face wouldn't be public) as they walked under the umbrella - and the mom smiled and said that would be fine.

Afterwards, I showed the mother and her daughter the photo I'd taken of them. And this is when the mother told me I'd actually taken their picture before. She reminded me that I'd shown them a picture of my granddaughter and told them my son and his wife (who is Vietnamese Australian) and my grandbaby were living in Australia, and *her* family (White father and Asian mother) reminded me of my son's family, and her little girl reminded me of my granddaughter. Seeing her sweet family together had brightened my heart that day – and seeing her and her daughter brightened my heart again today.

THEN I came upon a family - grandparents, I think, mother, father, and little boy - just starting their walk on the boardwalk from Boulevard Park. The little boy was in a rainsuit, and I said, "We should ALL be wearing those things!" And they laughed and agreed.

I turned around when I got to the park and started back up the boardwalk. The man with the brilliant smile waved as he approached - and I smiled and waved back like we were old friends. The little girl under the umbrella blew me a kiss as she and her mum walked past. And when I came upon the family of the boy in the rainsuit, I pointed to him and said, "He's the driest of ALL of us!" They laughed and nodded their heads. Someone in the family was asking someone else in the family if they could get a group photo and I volunteered to take it for them. "One, two three!" I said and clicked the cellphone they'd handed me. Then I thanked them for bringing me joy today with their little boy in the rainsuit.

What a sloshy, soggy, soppy, wonderful walk on the boardwalk this morning!

November 26, 2024

I ran some errands in downtown Mount Vernon today. The autumn displays are starting to be replaced by Christmas displays now: The autumn "trees" in Per Dona's display grabbed my eye and I had to take a quick snap; A block farther down there was a jolly Santa in the window.

I found Hunter (at the bottom of the ladder) and Aaron (top of the ladder) putting up the Christmas lights at the Skagit Valley Food Co-op. Both of them have worked there for years and enjoy being part of the Co-op family. Hunter asked me my name and I told him, then Aaron yelled down for me to repeat my name and I told him "like the meme." They both started laughing. Hunter told me that the "Karen" meme is starting to phase out now, and is being replaced by a "Jessica" meme. I did not know this, and felt my heart going out to all the Jessicas in the world.

The woman in front of me in the line at the Co-op realized she'd forgotten something when the cashier was checking her out, and she skipped out of line to go fetch whatever it was. She was quick and got back to the cashier before the cashier had finished scanning everything. I commended the customer for her speed. "Good job! You made it!" She laughed and thanked me. I told her that I usually forget the one thing I came in to get, and then I don't remember it until I get into the parking lot. She nodded her head and said she'd almost forgotten the thing her husband had asked her to fetch. She said he was going to be so happy she remembered.

I always love the trees in Pine Square in the autumn and wanted to snap a quick photo. I waited for a couple of young men to move past me before I raised my camera to take my picture. When I turned around, I realized one of the young men had turned to take a photo, too. It's always fun to meet other people who see the beauty

I see. "Did you get it?" I asked him. And he laughed and nodded his head.

Before I got back to my car, I passed a postal carrier and thanked him for his service. He grinned and laughed and thanked me back.

November 28, 2024

My brother Dave came up from Olympia to join us for Thanksgiving dinner today. Xander and Kyla were here, too, and Kyla's mom and dad, Deeann and Cedar, and her brother, Lyric. The dining room was full – full of people and laughter and conversation and savory food smells.

Thanksgiving is my favorite holiday. I love setting aside a day to express gratitude. I love the coming-together around the table. Our family tradition at Thanksgiving is to go around the table – from one person to the next – sharing what we're grateful for. That may be my favorite part of the holiday.

This Thanksgiving I'm grateful for a roof over our heads, food in our bellies, and clean water to drink. I'm grateful for family and friends, and I'm grateful that those of us sitting around the table were able to be together today. I remember a time not so long ago when the pandemic kept us separated and isolated from each other – a time when holidays were celebrated over Zoom and Skype. And I'm grateful we made it through that time to today.

December 8, 2024

I ran into one of my old boardwalk friends on my walk today. Dan asked me if I wanted to see his new friend and then he turned around and there was a puppy on his back! Awwww... that face! Dan, who is of Korean heritage, said his new friend had a Korean name – "Jakada" - and he said it means "little and cute" - which totally fits this sweet puppy!

I got a cocoa at the Boulevard Park coffee shop. I told Sunny, the barista, that it just seemed like a morning for cocoa - quiet and chilly and overcast.

Sunny agreed. Then she told me the night before she'd gone to the shabbat service at her Jewish temple and THEN gone to a Christmas party afterwards. I think Sunny was enjoying the quiet this morning.

December 9, 2024

Sign in 5b Bakery: "It's a good day to have a good day."

I drove up to the 5b Bakery in Concrete today, taking photos along the way. I always enjoy the staff and customers at the 5b – everyone is friendly and cheery. I also enjoy the food. I bought myself a banana waffle and sat down at a table by the window to do some people-watching.

A young couple came in with their baby girl. The baby was adorable! I was itching to get her photo, but in recent years I've become hesitant about taking pictures of children and posting them. So I didn't get a photo of her, but I did write a poem:

Fountain of hair on the top of her head,
she nestles safe in her mama's arms.
She turns her head to look at me
and I am instantly charmed.
I smile and wave and coo, "Hi, baby girl!"
and her face fills up with a grin.
Her eyes crinkle in the happy recognition
that she has found a new friend.

I stopped at the Burlington Fred Meyer on my way home. Mike "The-Best-Greeter-in-Skagit County" was at the door, festooned in his Christmas hat and ready with his welcoming smile.

When I brought my goods out to the parking lot I noticed a worm there, making his way across the asphalt by my car. How the poor little guy ended up in the parking lot I do not know, but it did not seem like a healthy place for him. So I picked him up and into my palm and carried him out to a nice field next to the parking lot, where I found a mole hole for him to nestle into.

It has been a good day for a good day: I saved a life; I had a 5b Bakery waffle; I exchanged smiles with a new little friend; and I was greeted by the best greeter in Skagit County.

December 17, 2024

Scott and I flew to California last weekend to see Andrew, Christina and Linh, and to visit other relatives who live near to them. It was a wonderful stay in every single way.

But, my friends, going into it, I had a lot of fear about it all. Would I get sick before we left and not be able to fly out? Would I get sick when I was down there and not be able to fly home? Would I lose my hearing aids? Would I lose my contact lens? Would I lose my passport? My cellphone? Would the plane lose a window mid-flight and would I get sucked through it kiester-first and get stuck in it? Would my grandbaby recognize me?

Fears like that.

I prayed about my fears and leaned into the shoulder of cosmic Love. I felt Love wrapping me up in Her arms and giving me a big hug. Love never changes, never ends, never abandons us. Love loves us even when we're being ridiculous.

The four days of our trip flew by. Here are the highlights:

Jose, our shuttlebus driver from the parking lot to SeaTac Airport was so cool! He's from Nicaragua and was singing a song from Ecuador. Jose said we're all on this planet to help one another, and I said, "We're all in this together!" He grinned and nodded his head and sang us his songs. What a great way to start the day.

The flight out was a little rocky – there were a couple of big bumps that would have sent us flying out of our seats if we hadn't been buckled in – but everyone was so matter-of-fact about it all. The man across the aisle from me was calmly eating his snacks, and watching a movie on his cellphone as our plane tossed and bucked. I thanked him for that, and he smiled back at me – completely at ease with our wild ride.

When we landed we found our rental car and let *Mrs. Google* direct us to Andrew and Christina's place. I hurried ahead of Scott – eager to see our granddaughter. I peeked around the curtain and into the living room, and there she was! She looked up and saw me and her whole face lit up in a grin! She recognized me! Pretty soon she was toddle-running to the door and pretty soon I had her in my arms again. Oh, joy! Oh, wonder!

I was reading a book to Linh and there was a picture of a pizza piece in it. We'd just had pizza the night before and Linh had bitten into a jalapeno – which she tried to blow out in the same way you'd blow out a candle. "Pfft pfft." Now, as she saw the illustration of the piece of pizza, she pointed to it and pointed to her mouth and then said, "Pfft pfft."

As I was reading *Good night, Gorilla* to Linh, I was describing to her what the gorilla was doing in the illustrations, "The gorilla stole the zookeeper's keys and now he's letting ALL the animals out of their cages, and look – they're following the zookeeper back to his home." Linh pointed to the keys in the picture and pointed to the door and turned her little hand like she was opening the door with the keys. When I mentioned this to Christina, she told me that Linh has been trying to open the doors with her keys, but it hasn't worked out for her – she keeps dropping them. Later I joined Andrew for a walk with Linh, and he let her carry his keys. When we got to the gate, he helped her unlock it. She was so proud and pleased with herself!

Christina and I took Linh to the park. I helped Linh climb up to the top of the slide and helped her get situated so she could slide down to her mum. When she got to the bottom she turned around with a big grin on her face, and pointed to me and then to the slide, letting me know she wanted me to go down the slide now. So I did.

A few hours later I was reading a book to her that included a picture of a slide. She pointed to the slide and then pointed to me and then pointed back to the slide. She was reminding me that I had gone down the slide, too!

I read a story that included a bunny. I pointed to the bunny's ears, and Linh pointed to her own ears, and then pointed to my ears and pointed back to the bunny's ears again. She got up and toddled over to Christina and pointed to her mum's ears and then she toddled to Scott to point to his ears. And pretty son Grandpa Scott was teaching her the "Head and shoulders, knees and toes" song.

Andrew and Christina guided us on a walk to the Larchmont neighborhood where there were all kinds of cool shops and bakeries. We made stops at a couple of bakeries where Andrew bought us vegan treats.

There was also a great   Mexican bakery, K Bakery, right across the street from our motel where we bought smoothies and little fruit-filled turnovers to begin our day. I loved the atmosphere in there – lively Mexican music playing in the background, and paintings by Mexican artists on the wall, and everyone friendly and helpful.

Scott's sister's daughter, Kate, and her husband, Tan, live about half an hour from Andrew and Christina. We took advantage of this by paying them a visit on our second day in California. It was so good to see them again, and to enjoy watching our grandbaby playing with Kate and Tan's little ones. Both Christina and Tan are of Vietnamese heritage, and it seemed perfect for Tan to order take-out from a nearby Vietnamese restaurant. The food was great; the fellowship with family was dear; and watching the little ones playing together brought me a heart full of grins. It was a perfect visit.

We spent our last night with my cousin, Laurie, and her husband, Roger, and their son, James. I hadn't seen Laurie since my dad's hundredth birthday six years ago and it meant so much to me to be able to connect with her again. Her daughter, Allison, came over with her young daughter and it was good to be able to be able to see them again, too, and get caught up on life.

Laurie brought out some old family photos that she inherited from her mom and some of our aunts, and we went looking through them together, talking about our family history, and sharing memories.

Our last day in California, Cousin Laurie drove Scott and I to the coast and I got to dip my toes in the Pacific.

We met these two very cool fishermen at a marina near the ocean. I asked Rafael if I could take his photo, and he had no problems with that. I asked him his name and he said Rafael, and then he asked me mine. "Karen, of course," I said, grinning. He laughed with me about my name – successfully passing my "Karen Test."

Philip was relaxing in his chair on the other side of the pier, classic rock playing from his e-bike. He'd overheard me introduce myself to Rafael and, smiling, told me I did that "right." "You gotta have fun with it, right?" I said, laughing.

Philip told us that he once caught the biggest angel shark ever seen in the harbor – he said it was about five and a half feet long and four feet wide! He took a picture of it before it went back into the water. Philip also told us that we could find him on his *YouTube* channel, "Honey Hole Trackers."

I asked Philip and Rafael if they were old friends, and they said they'd just met that day. I told them I had a feeling this was the beginning of a long friendship.

The day before, when I'd said goodbye to Linh before we headed to Laurie's, my grandbaby had put her little arms around my neck and clung to me and sobbed, and I'd sobbed, too. I didn't want our last goodbye before we left California to be a repeat of that. I worried about it. And I prayed.

We took a last walk around the block with Andrew and our granddaughter – posing under the golden autumn leaves of the gingko tree across the street, stopping to touch tree bark and wave to dogs going on walks with their humans. When we were done with our walk we went back inside Andrew and Christina's home and read books. Andrew started beating on the toy tambourine that had been one of my first gifts to the baby, and then Andrew handed me the tambourine and he began to shake a rattle in time to my beats, and we sang and made a song together. Pretty soon Linh started dancing to our song. Her dance was charming and filled my grandma's heart.

When Scott started putting on his shoes, Linh brought me my shoes to put on, too. Scott and I gathered our things to leave. Linh reached up for a hug, and I asked her to kiss my cheek (I pointed to it), and then kiss my other cheek, too, and she smiled and put her little face next to me. We hugged Christina and Andrew goodbye, and then I transferred Linh to Andrew and he turned her the other direction, and Scott and I slipped out the door. As we left, we looked up at their window, and Linh was at the window with Andrew and Christina waving goodbye to us and smiling. We waved goodbye back and smiled and blew everyone a kiss. It was a sweet, joyful parting. Perfect!

Our flight home was at night. *Mrs. Google* led us through Hollywood – we didn't even realize we were IN Hollywood until we saw the Hollywood Museum sign. That was cool. There was heavy traffic getting to the airport, but once we got there everything went pretty quickly. There was no one in front of us at the TSA screening desk, and we got through all of that smoothly. We chatted to a delightful fellow passenger named Samantha in the waiting area – Samantha was going home to Seattle to be with her family over the holidays.

We boarded our flight, buckled ourselves in, and two and half hours later we were back in the rain of Seattle.

Note: I did not lose my passport, my contact lens, or my hearing aids; I did not get sucked out of the plane; and I did not get sick. Love deposited me gently back in my home after a lovely visit with my family. And here we are.

December 22, 2024

I haven't been on the boardwalk for more than a week and missed my walk something terrible. I asked Scott if he'd join me on the boardwalk, and soon we were ambling in my "happy place." It felt so good to be back there!

Just as Scott and I were starting our walk, we met Murphy in the Village Green. His humans were sitting on a bench on the edge of the Green and Murphy was standing in front of them, totally focused on them. There was something about his stance that put a grin on my face, and I asked if I could come up and give him a pet. His humans smiled and said sure. Murphy turned to me when he saw me coming, and wagged his tail in welcome. Such a sweet pup!

We hadn't gone much farther on our walk when I saw another pup, little Max, with a whole miniature Christmas Village affixed to his back! So cute!

As we were coming down the ramp to Taylor Dock we saw a couple of folks about to jump into the bay. Tommy and Hannah agreed to let us take their photo as they jumped. Brave souls.

And then we met a sweet pup named Cal, who was escorting his little family down the boardwalk. I asked if I could get Cal's photo, and his human graciously agreed. Cal was so chill! His human said he was born chill.

We took the stairs up to the top of the little knoll. As we were walking to the other side, a little Downy Woodpecker flitted into the trees and landed on a trunk. It was moving too quickly to get a good picture, but it brought me a smile anyway.

After our walk, I treated Scott to an early lunch at the Colophon. The hostess who seated us sang out her welcome, and I said, "And this one sings!" She grinned and said that, on top of that, her name was Noelle! "The first Noelle..." I sang, and she laughed.

It was so good to be back on the boardwalk today. I really needed that.

December 27, 2024

I had a soul-filling walk in Bellingham today. I met a sweet pup named Sunshine; caught sight of a jaunty little foot ferry peeking out from behind some other boats near the road; found a tree that was still holding onto colorful autumn leaves in its branches; enjoyed watching a schooner glide along the water; and took photos of boat reflections.

I waved to a familiar face from the boardwalk when I saw her walking through Boulevard Park and she smiled and waved back. We only know each other from our walks, but she feels like an old friend to me now. I saw her again, walking in front of me, as I headed back to my car. When she looked behind her and saw me, she slowed down so we could walk together for a bit.

We talked about our favorite Bellingham walks - the boardwalk and Lake Padden. I asked her if she was a hiker - she looked to me like someone I might run into on a mountain trail someday. And this is when I learned my old friend from the boardwalk had actually taken a trek to the base of Annapurna in her younger days. Which. Whoah. I told her then about my dad, Dee Molenaar (because of course I did) who is in *Wikipedia* for mountain climbing. I told her about the 1953 expedition to K2 he was on, and the watercolor he painted at 25,000' on K2. I told her I'd climbed to the summits of Rainier and Baker, Adams and Hood, with Dad when I was younger. And she told me that when she moved to Seattle in 1962, she wished she'd joined the Seattle Mountaineers. I told her my pop had been a member of the Mountaineers for years.

As often happens with my old friends from the boardwalk, I don't actually know their names. I thought that maybe she was "Mary" - but I wasn't sure. I asked her her name and was told that she was indeed "Mary" and then she asked mine and I told her "Karen."

Mary and I agreed that it's important to keep our bodies moving. We may be slower than we once were, and we may not be climbing large mountains these days, but we're still moving.

I hope I see Mary again soon on the boardwalk.

It hit me today as I was
hanging another ornament on the tree -
a gift from east coast family -
that no matter how many ornaments I hang
I'm never going to have
my whole family together again
in the person, on this planet.
Parents have passed now; Loved ones scattered.
And somehow facing this reality
and accepting it -
helped give me perspective on what matters.
I'd been raising the bar too high for Christmas -
making my joy dependent on what can't be -
instead of being grateful for all the good that IS -
for all the good that's mine here and now.
There's still so much to celebrate -
and nothing can separate
me from the love of Love Itself.

December 28, 2024

I'd just told Scott that I hadn't seen Lucy walking in the neighborhood lately. I was worried about her. Right after that, a friend texted to let me know that Lucy was in the hospital and didn't have much time left. Scott and I went in to see her this morning.

Lucy smiled at us when we came in, her blue eyes twinkling with humor. When I started talking about what we would do when she got out of the hospital, she smiled and looked me directly in the eyes. "No, this is it," she said, with her Irish lilt. "It's almost done now. I'm ready." She knew she was dying, and she was at peace with it.

I started tearing up.

"Lucy, I love you. I want you to know you've made a difference to our community," I told her. "You're dear to me."

"And you're dear to *me*," Lucy said, her eyes focused on mine.

Scott said his good byes to Lucy, and we hugged her.

As soon as I got out into the hall I broke down and started sobbing. I know I'll never again see Lucy walking the streets of Bow. She may be ready for her death, but I don't know if I am.

December 29, 2024

And now a poem:

A trio of pups smiling at me -
Cedar, Rufus, and Arlo
(like Guthrie) -
and a smiling toddler peering
at the birds in the bay below.
His family's laughter is contagious.
I find myself laughing as I follow
them down the ramp to the dock
and the boardwalk.
It starts raining. I put up my hood
and I head for Wood's.
Today I have a free cup of coffee
coming to me.
I drink my breve and listen to
the humansong -
voices old and young -
enveloping me in a bubble
of cheer.
It's cozy in here.
I venture to the other side of the park,
rescuing worms from the sidewalk
as I go.
And then I head back towards Fairhaven.
I get in conversation
with another shutterbug
and we talk about birds we've seen
in the course of our photographing.
The rain is pouring now
and I lift my face to the deluge
and wonder who invented the hood.

December 31, 2024

What a remarkable day!

I was tempted to just stay home ensconced in my comfy chair by the woodstove. But I roused myself out of the chair and headed to Lake Padden instead.

And I'm so glad I did!

Not long after I'd started walking the trail a woman coming from the other direction smiled at me and her eyes lit up in recognition. "Are you Karen?" she asked. I nodded my head, and she started talking about my photos on *Facebook* and I realized this was my friend, Li Hua! Li and I have been friends on *Facebook* for years, I think, but I'd never actually met her in the person before! It was cosmic to run into her here at Lake Padden on the last day of the year - I'd always hoped that someday we'd meet. Li Hua is an incredible photographer, and we talked for a bit about our shared love for taking photos, and spending time in nature. We exchanged a hug and phone numbers and wished each other a happy new year. Joy!

I hadn't gone much farther when I saw Mary coming towards me. You may remember that I wrote a couple of days ago about meeting Mary on the boardwalk - she's the woman who hiked to the base of Annapurna in her younger days. We'd shared mountaineering stories, and we'd talked about our favorite walks in Bellingham - the boardwalk and Lake Padden - and here she was at Lake Padden! I told her I was trying to stockpile happy memories for the "interesting" year we have ahead of us, and she started grinning at that. She observed that "interesting" was a good word for what appears to be coming down the pike. It was so good to see Mary's smile again.

I continued on my walk and now a young woman with a little preschooler looked up and saw me and stopped on the trail. "Are you Mrs. Terrell?" she asked. And there was Kristine - one of my former eighth graders! We exchanged hugs and smiles, and I felt my heart fill up with happy memories of being Kristine's teacher.

But wait! There's more!

Back in November I ordered new contact lenses from my optometrist's office. In December I stopped by the office to see if they'd arrived, yet, and learned that, because of a change in personnel in the doctor's office, they'd never been ordered. I was told they should arrive within the week. I didn't hear anything, so I stopped by last week to see if they'd come in, and was told they hadn't, yet.

When I left Lake Padden, I decided I had time to drive to the optometrist's office and see if there was any word about the contacts. I was thinking that if the lenses hadn't come in, I would just ask them to cancel the order and see if I could order them myself. When I got to the office it looked like they were closed. But then I saw that the side office - the one that sends out orders for glasses and lenses was open - so I went in there.

There were a handful of young people manning the shop - all friendly and helpful. I told my story to the receptionist behind the counter, and she asked me for my last name and then my first. "I am, of course, Karen," I told her, smiling. "I am Karen and I want to talk to your manager." The receptionist started laughing then and clicked things into her computer. She told me that she had "thousands" of boxes of contact lenses in the windowed room behind the counter and she was going to take a look and see what she could find.

I could watch her through the windows as she looked through the boxes of contact lenses, and, as one after another of the boxes got set aside, I was beginning to lose hope. And then I saw that moment when she found them!

She brought them out and matched up the numbers on the boxes with the prescription in her computer and confirmed these were mine. I asked her if I needed to pay anything - and she looked at her computer and then told me that my insurance had covered everything. I told her she was an angel and finding my contact lenses had been a miracle for me - I was down to my last contact lens!

On the drive into the optometrist's office I'd passed a field of trumpeter swans. I stopped by the field now and snapped some quick photos of swans doing swan things.

It has been a good last day of 2024.

January 1, 2025

Scotty and I celebrated the New Year with a hike at Whatcom Falls Park. We met way cool pups; discovered trails we'd never been on before; and saw moss. A lot of moss. Many mosses. Thick and velvety and dripping from the trees and wrapping everything in emerald.

I met new tree-friends - cedars and Doug firs and hemlocks. Scott and I posed behind some of our new tree-friends while new human-friends, Hope and Luke, snapped pictures of us.

We wound our way down soft mulchy paths through the evergreens, stopping to take pictures of smiling pups and mossy things, until we eventually meandered back to the Falls.

As we were heading back to our car we passed a group of lively young people - maybe friends from WWU? - with wet hair and towels around their shoulders. I had to ask, right? "Did you just jump into the creek?" I asked a young woman with rainbow hair. She grinned and nodded. I asked her if it was her first time jumping in the water, and she said no, but it was her first time doing it in winter. Whoah. Jumping into that white water during summer would have been daring enough - but doing it in winter?! I told her I was impressed, and she laughed - I think she was kind of impressed with what she'd just done, too - and we wished each other a happy New Year.

January 4, 2025

Such a nice group of people waiting in the Starbucks line at Fred Meyer's today. My friend, Gabriel, was manning the counter today, and I let everyone in line know that they were in good hands with Gabriel. The couple in the front of the line took a sip of their drinks when Gabriel handed it to them, and the woman turned to me and smiled and let me know I was right - Gabriel had done a good job with it. When it came my turn to pick up my mocha, Gabriel came out from behind the counter to give me a hug. I really needed that hug today. Thank you, Gabriel!

January 9, 2025

I got up early this morning and by 10:00 I was feeling ready to go back to bed. But it was so beautiful outside. And it seemed a waste to sleep when I could be outside exchanging smiles with people and pups. I wasn't sure, exactly, where I was going to end up, but I decided to get into my car and find out where Life led me.

I ended up at Boulevard Park and decided to walk from there to downtown. On my way to the trail, I thought I recognized two of my friends from the boardwalk, Rob and Coleen. "I know you, right?" I asked, and Coleen smiled and confirmed this, and we exchanged a hug. I told Rob he was doing important work with his interviews on his *YouTube* channel, "Old Man in the Park." Rob said it was just a hobby, but I told him what he was doing was important and needed - connecting with people and listening to them. I think the world needs more of that.

I started up the trail and hadn't gone far when this little pup named Luna started wagging her tail and smiling at me. I gave her a scratch behind the ears and her human let me take her picture. Sweetness!

A little farther on and I exchanged smiles and greetings with someone garbed in fishnet stockings, a long brown coat, a purple hat, and glasses. Their smile was so open and friendly, and their eyes so full of kindness, that the power of their greeting just filled me all up with cosmic goodness.

I'd almost reached downtown when Luna and her human passed me again - this time going the other direction - and I got to exchange one more smile before we passed.

I got to the corner in front of the big public parking lot and held back on the sidewalk, planning to just wait for all the cars to get through the intersection before I crossed. But the folks in this one car stopped and waved for me to cross over. I grinned and shook my head and gave them a big traffic controller wave to go ahead. They laughed and passed through the intersection, and we all waved at each other and smiled. I love polite people.

I decided to stop in at the Wood's coffee shop and get myself a mocha and a scone. The baristas there were very cool. One started making my drink, while the other manned the cash register. The young man at the register fed me my line: "What would be a good name for this?" he asked.

I know my cue when I hear it. "Well, I don't know if it's a good name, but my name is Karen," I told him. He started laughing and said he was sorry about the Karen meme. I gave him a nice tip for that.

When I got back on the trail to Boulevard Park, I saw the person in the fishnet stockings and brown coat coming my way again. I started grinning as soon as I saw them. When I got to them, I said, "We're old friends now!" and they laughed and said that we were, indeed. And it occurred to me that the first time I meet someone we're new friends, but by the second time we're already old friends.

A woman who'd passed me earlier passed me again going the other direction. She smiled and wished me a good day, and I wished her the same. But then I immediately thought, why stop with the day? "Have a good YEAR!" I said, and she laughed and wished me a good year, too.

Not long after, I saw something rustling in the branches to the side of the trail. I turned to look at what was going on there. That's when I saw a squirrel running along the branches of the trees into a holly bush. I was fascinated by his antics and watched him as he snipped off a sprig of holly berries with his teeth and scampered back into the woods. I had no idea squirrels liked holly berries!

When I got back to Boulevard Park, I heard a familiar voice coming from off to my right. And there was my dear friend,

Rebecca! "Rebecca!" I called. She turned, and her sweet pup, Bear, came running to greet me.

Rebecca and I sat in the sun under the roof of the little amphitheater in the park and talked and laughed for maybe an hour. Finding her in the park this afternoon was just exactly what I needed to complete my day. She is a treasure of a human being.

A man walking by overheard us laughing and turned around and asked if it would be okay if he used one of our phones to take our photo. Rebecca handed him her phone and he snapped a picture, and then I asked him if I could get a picture of HIM. So that happened.

I'm so glad I decided not to go back to bed.

January 10, 2025

The son and his family are in LA
and I've been feeling disquieted -
feeling the distance
as the fires burn between us.

But tonight I went in search
of the sunset and I remembered
other sunsets and my son and I
hopping in the car to find them.

I mentally bring my son
with me now in my hunt
to find reflections of pink clouds
in flooded fields
and I feel his energy around me -
joyful and free.

I find a glorious sunset
and my heart finds peace.
Then my son messages me that
at the end of the day
he went in search of the sunset, too,
from his home in LA.

January 12, 2025

I saw my old friend, Dan, with his new pup-friend, Jakada. The last time I saw Jakada she was a tiny fluff of fur in Dan's backpack. Now she's a slightly bigger fluff of fur and she let me pet her under her chin.

I saw two young men heading for Taylor Dock with towels over their shoulders and asked them if they were going in. They confirmed this. They said they made a resolution to do this every week - and this is now their third jump. They agreed to let me take a photo of them as they jumped into the briny deep. I asked them for their names afterwards, and the first jumper introduced himself as "Elliot" - I told him that was one of my favorite names. The second jumper introduced himself as "Hewson" (sp?) and I told him I'd never heard that name before. I decreed they both had superlative names, and my name - "Karen" - is one of the best of all. Elliot and Hewson got a good laugh out of that.

January 13, 2025

Fred's this morning:

There's a man looking at the Odwalla juices. He's taking his time picking out the just right juices for himself. I'm enjoying his process. He picks up one, then picks up another, sort of weighs them back and forth in his hands, looks at the labels - and I get it - making choices can be hard.

His cart is parked in front of the mushrooms. I want to bag some mushrooms for myself, but I don't want to interrupt his process. He looks to have made his choice now, though, so I start to move in on the mushrooms, and then he changes his mind. I say, "Can I just reach in here...?" He looks up and starts laughing, and apologizes to me. I'm laughing, too. "No, no, it's fine. I just want to..." And he smiles back at me and apologizes again and makes his juice choices and moves on.

A few minutes later I connect with him again in another aisle - this time he's apologizing to another man - I think he was accidentally blocking the aisle or something. I start laughing and say, "Are you causing trouble again?" Both men start cracking up. There's this quick moment of shared laughter, and I soak it up. I really needed to laugh with people today.

I'm ready to check out. I'm trying to determine which line might go faster. I start to go into one line and then peek over at the other line - it looks a little shorter.   I catch the eyes of another customer in that line and he grins. I give him the thumbs up and move into his line behind him. He's holding two avocadoes. "Is that all you've got?" I ask him. And he laughs and explains that he would have gone through the self-checkout, but the avocadoes are missing their tags and he doesn't want to deal with that, so he's just going to wait for an actual clerk to check him out.

As we're talking, the woman in front of him turns around and invites him to go in front of her with his two avocadoes. I start talking to the woman now - chatting about the old express lanes they used to have at Fred's in the olden days – and, when I look back, I see that the man with two avocadoes has now been invited by the next customer in front of him to move to the front of the line. How cool!

The woman bagging my groceries is giving the cashier cheerful grief - they have a back-and-forth bantering going on that tells me they enjoy each other. The cashier grumbles some good-natured thing about the bagger, and I say, "She's in fine form today." The cashier and bagger both start cracking up.

I leave Fred's with a smile on my face.

I can't imagine my life without people who know how to laugh with me.

January 15, 2025

Today I met up with two remarkable women, Deidre and Rosemary, at Restrettos. We shared inspiration and laughter, the good things in our lives and the challenges. I felt all warmed by the glow of my friends' kindness and love.

Rosemary had to leave for an appointment,   Not long after she left a young woman with a cane came in and sat at the table next to ours. I moved a chair out of her way to make it easier for her to get around us and she thanked me.

I saw her taking pictures of the paintings in the shop and asked her if she was an artist. She smiled and said no, but she really liked museums. Deidre and I introduced ourselves and we learned her name was Jen. Her friend Jeannie soon joined her, and we got in a conversation about museums we'd visited. We discovered we'd all seen Picasso's original artwork at some point!

I saw Jeannie was wearing a Seahawks scarf and told her I liked it. Jen said she'd bought that scarf for Jeannie for her birthday last week, and we wished Jeannie a happy birthday.

When Deidre and I got up to leave, Jen thanked us for the conversation, and we thanked her and Jeannie in turn. For me, meeting new friends is one of Life's biggest joys.

And now I'm sitting here, remembering that during the Pandemic we wouldn't have been able to come together like that. I'm so grateful for what we have right now. So grateful for time together with old friends, and the opportunity to meet new ones.

January 18, 2025

I parked near the Alaska Ferry Terminal in Fairhaven this morning and did some meandering around the terminal and Marine Park and then up to the Village Green.

I waved to one of the workers on the Alaska Ferry and he smiled and waved back; I discovered that one of the trees near the terminal is one of the oldest Empress trees in America; I found a place where people can rent kayaks in Marine Park and filed that away for future reference; and I stopped in at the Fairhaven Coffee shop along the way for a chocolate croissant and a mocha, and a chat with one of my favorite baristas, Kenzie.

Kenzie is studying to become a social studies teacher, and, because I was a social studies teacher for many years, I have a lot of fun talking with her about social studies teacher stuff. She is going to be a FANTASTIC teacher! Yesterday we talked about historical fiction books that can be used in social studies classes. And then - because it became obvious she is an avid reader - I took a leap and guessed she's probably a writer, too. And she is!

So then we talked about writing for a while. Kenzie told me about a book she's working on - a fantasy fiction that sounds AMAZING! I could totally see it being made into a movie - or a movie series. And I told Kenzie that she is actually IN the book I'm working on right now - a book that will be the third book in my *Cosmic Celebrations* series. It was such a kick to meet a fellow bibliophile and writer - AND a fellow social studies teacher!

After my walk in Fairhaven, I went to the Burlington Fred Meyer's for groceries.

My favorite wild blueberries were on sale! There was only one bag left and I snatched it up. There were five bottles left of blueberry juice - also on sale - and I nabbed four of 'em and brought the fifth one up to the front of the shelf so it was easy to see. I imagined some other blueberry juice aficionado finding that last bottle and I smiled.

I ran into old friends, Gale and Jon, and we exchanged hugs and got caught up with each other. Gale was one of the first people I met when my husband and I moved here in 1985 - so we've known each other almost 40 years! Whoah. There's something really beautiful about being able to connect with old friends in these unplanned, spontaneous moments.

I wheeled my groceries to the end of the checkout line and looked around me to find people to exchange smiles with. There was a mother with her two daughters standing at the end of the line next to me. When I glanced in her cart I saw that she had two bags of those wild blueberries! I lifted my bag out of my cart to show her MY bag o' blueberries and she smiled. She said when she saw they were on sale she'd grabbed two - and I thanked her for leaving the last bag for me. Then we talked for a moment about the glories of wild blueberries.

A man pushed his cart into the line behind me. He was wearing a WSU Cougar cap. I asked him what year he'd graduated from WSU and he said '73. I told him I'd graduated in '78. I asked him if George Raveling had been there when he was there and he nodded his head. (George Raveling was one of my favorite people at WSU when I was there.) Then we talked about the changes in the PAC-12 and the transfer portal that sucked up WSU's quarterback and coach before our big bowl game. We both agreed that we were proud of what our Cougs were able to pull off in that bowl game, despite the loss of key people.

The cashier began ringing up my groceries, and the bagger brought out a plastic bag to start bagging them in. I asked her not to use the plastic bag - and suggested she just use the bag I'd brought in - put the small stuff in there - and the big stuff she could put directly in the cart. Then I apologized. "I'm sorry. I'm being bossy."

The bagger and the cashier both started laughing, and, nodding to the bagger, the cashier said, "SOMEone's got to take charge of her!" I told them I loved them - told them I come into Fred's for the laughs. This got them laughing some more and we all wished each other a good day.

After I'd paid for my groceries, I rolled my cart down to the in-store Starbucks. Gabriel was manning the counter today, and we had a chance to talk before another customer joined the queue. I observed that he had a great voice and asked him if he was a singer in his second job - he said no, but his mom had been a trained opera singer. I told him my mom had been trained for opera, too! So that was cool. And then he told me all about what he and his husband are doing to get their new apartment ready to move into - the move is soon! I'm so happy for him. Before I left, he came around the counter and gave me a hug and thanked me for making him feel so welcome in his new community.

Fred's is known for its "one-stop shopping" - but, for me, our local Fred's is more than that. It's a community meeting place; a social hub; a place to connect with old friends and new. A place to find people to laugh with.

January 22, 2025

The boardwalk was calling me today, so I bundled up and drove to Fairhaven for a walk in the frost and the sun.

And something amazing happened up there this morning. (I know, when DOESN'T something amazing happen up there, right?) In fact, something amazing just happened right NOW that ties into that other something amazing.

I'd started at Boulevard Park this time - ran into my old friend Dan (with his puppy, Jakada, peeking out of his backpack) and stopped for a quick chat. Soon after running into Dan, I saw another boardwalk friend, Mary, coming down the path and called out a greeting to her. We exchanged smiles and happy banter about the dazzling day. Just seeing her again lifted my heart.

When I got to the ramp from Taylor Dock I saw that it was icy. I smiled at a woman of about my age who was cautiously making her way down the ramp. I told her I'm careful coming down the ramp, too, on days like this. She grinned back at me and happily pointed out she'd almost made it to the bottom. Several groups of people were coming down the ramp Australia-style - they were coming down on the left side because it wasn't as icy there. As they got closer to me, I moved over to the middle so they could get by. One of the people thanked me for moving over, and I told her that I knew on my return trip I'd be going down on the left side, too. This made her laugh.

When I got up to Fairhaven Green, I saw a poster about a concert my friend, Tracy Spring, is going to be giving at the end of the month. How fun to see my friend smiling back at me from that poster!

I decided to check out Village Books to see if any books leaped off the shelves at me and begged to be taken home. There were a couple of young men standing in front of the sci-fi/fantasy section, looking at a book called *Under the Whispering Door*. One of the men was describing how fun this book was to his friend. I, of course, had to cut in on them to find out more. We all introduced ourselves and I learned the young man who'd read *Under the Whispering Door* was Danny, and his friend was Patrick. They were good sports about letting me take their photo, and Danny was very persuasive about that book. I ended up buying myself a copy.

I got myself a "sippy hot chocolate" (thick European-style cocoa) at Evolve, the cafe on the top of the bookstore, and sat by the window to drink it.

As I was sitting there, my social-studies-teacher noggin picked up on the conversation coming from a table in the corner. I heard the young man sitting at the table tell an older man sitting across from him that he was interested in studying "global affairs" and working as a humanitarian in countries that were struggling with things like a lack of clean water and food. I heard the older man use the words "Wall Street" and I heard the younger man say that he wasn't really interested in working on Wall Street - that wasn't really what he was passionate about. Then he talked about a game called "GeoGuessr" - an online game that uses *Google* photos to put you in some random place in the world and you have to guess where you are. That sounded like a very cool game to me.

When I finished my cocoa, and was ready to leave, I had to stop by their table and talk to the young man with the humanitarian heart. I told the pair that I was a former social studies teacher, and I'd picked up on words they were using in their conversation - "global affairs" and "humanitarian" - and had been listening in. I told the young man - who introduced himself as Miles - that listening to him had given me hope for the world. The other man - who introduced himself as Marty - asked me if I was going to write about meeting them, and I asked Miles and Marty if it was alright for me to do that. They both agreed that would be fine.

Which leads me to this amazing thing that JUST happened: A woman named Grace just messaged me: "Hi Karen, This might be a weird question, but were you at Evolve Cafe this morning? (I think you met my son, who was being interviewed for college.)"

Isn't that COSMIC?!!!

But there's more! Grace let me know that when she relayed the story of my meeting Miles to her partner, her partner (who is a geologist) let her know that he'd used an illustration by my dad (who was also a geologist) in one of his books. Whoah.

I love all these connections we have with one another. I love our kinship. I love our cosmic community.

January 24, 2025

Just when I begin to sink into despair, something happens that fills me all up with joy and hope. It's only noon, and already my day has been filled with Good, with the recognition that nothing - absolutely NOTHING - can stop Love from reaching us and blessing us.

A really remarkable thing happened this morning right after I got myself out of bed and dressed. (I had considered just staying there for another hour or two - but this voice told me to get up - that something good was coming!) There was a knock on the door and Scott went to answer it. I heard him talking to a woman, and then I heard him ask the woman if she wanted to talk to me.

I went to the door and saw one of my former eighth graders standing there! Diana had been in my first class of eighth graders in Burlington - back in 1992! I hadn't seen her for maybe twenty or thirty years! She told me that she's living in Minnesota now, but she's home to visit her mom, and she just had to stop in and see me.

And pretty soon we were hugging and crying and it was such a beautiful coming together that my heart just filled up with joy. Diana told me that she'd been wanting to write me, but the words just never came, so she'd decided to talk to me in the person. She told me that her eighth-grade year with me had been the most important year in her life and it had stayed with her. She said I'd made a difference in her life - that I'd treated all of my students like I was their mother, and I'd nurtured them like they were my children. She said she'd never had that from a teacher before and it had meant something to her, and she wanted me to know that.

She remembered at the beginning of the school year, when I'd invited all the parents and students in to meet me, how I'd walked around with my baby (Andrew would have been about nine months

129

then) on my back, and how he'd burped up baby stuff on my shoulder, and how I'd laughed about it. That had made an impression on her - she said she'd never met another teacher like me before.

Diana was a gift from the Cosmos this morning. The love in our space was palpable.

"Despair not; for Love IS with thee."

Kyla invited me to their house today for tea and cake.

Xander and Kyla's tiny cat, Olive, was stretched out in the sun on a soft chair, and let me scratch her behind her ears. Their more substantial cat, Nubi, was nowhere to be found – she's pretty shy – but I called out a greeting to her wherever she was hiding. Kyla says the cats are really enjoying their new home – there's a lot more space for them to explore and they seem to like being on the ground level where they can sit on the windowsills and watch the doings of the neighborhood.

I love what Kyla's done with their place! She's filled it with bright, warm colors, comfortable furniture, and cozy spaces to sit and chat.

We drank tea and ate home-made lemon-blueberry cake at the long dining room table Kyla found at a used furniture store. We got caught up on family and friends and adventures, and, inevitably, laughed together at the absurdities of life

I'm so glad Kyla and I are kin. I need every person in my life who helps me laugh.

January 25, 2025

What a lovely day in Bellingham! I parked at Boulevard Park and walked the boardwalk up to Fairhaven. I ran into my old friends, Dan and Jakada Pup, and little Hans (looking very dapper in his puppy jacket).

I had a yearning to go to Tony's Coffee Shop, and found myself mourning its loss again today. But I decided to go to the Cafe Blue and check it out. And oh, it was AWESOME there! It was full of young people - laughing and reading and talking - and I just let that youthful energy wrap around me. I realized that I've really missed being around young people since I retired from teaching several years ago.

I think I was probably the oldest one in Cafe Blue this morning and felt a little self-conscious about my gray hair. But I stepped up to the counter and presented myself to Micah, the barista, and he made me feel right at home. I asked him if it was okay for me to be there with my gray hair and he started laughing and told me of course! I asked for a mocha and a cookie called a rosamaria. I told Micah I'd never had a rosamaria cookie before - and he grinned and told me this was going to change my life. Micah asked me what I was taking photos of today, and I told him pups and birds and people, and, in fact, could I take his picture? He graciously smiled for me and let me snap a photo.

It was pretty packed in the cafe, but I found a couch in the corner that wasn't occupied. There was a young man in the corner, sitting in a chair reading a book, and I asked him if it was alright to sit there. He smiled and said sure, and I plopped myself down on the sofa.

Pretty soon a group of friends came to the corner looking for somewhere to sit, and I moved down - closer to the man with the book - to make room for this new group.

I got into conversation with the man in the chair. I learned his name is True and he asked me my name. "Get this," I said, grinning, "my name is Karen." He started laughing at that. I found out that True is a student at Seattle U., and he's in Bellingham to visit his brother. I learned he's majoring in philosophy, and I told him I'd really enjoyed my one philosophy class in graduate school - it had made me think, and that's always a good thing. True mentioned that Seattle University - like probably most schools right now - is focusing on their STEM program. "STEM is important," I said, "but we need the other stuff, too, the 'soul' stuff - art and music and English and philosophy." True nodded his head in agreement and said we need the things that tell us "why." I really like how he phrased that.

True let me take his photo before I left. We wished each other a good day, and I headed back to Boulevard Park, feeling all filled up with the joy of hanging out with young folks for a while.

January 28, 2025

I just went for a walk in the 'hood. It feels like springtime out there: The sun is shining; the birds are winging; things are starting to bud.

I walked by Lucy's house and the image of her sweet smile and twinkling blue eyes popped into my head. I stopped and chatted with Brenda and Tracy for a bit. I waved as I went by Linda's house. Virginia was walking around the neighborhood with her little ones, and we waved to each other. Jeff drove by in his truck and smiled and waved back to me.

I'm grateful for this little spot of kindness and community. As we head into the next few years, I think community is going to become more and more valuable to the world.

January 29, 2025

When I went out to my car this morning, I had the vagueish (vagueish is, like, EXTRA vague) idea I was going to head to Bellingham for a walk. But by the time I was turning the key in the ignition I'd seen the oil change sticker on my window and realized that today I should get my oil changed.

So I drove to the Valvoline in Burlington and parked my car in the line. A man named Jeremy came out to check me in. I immediately liked him. He smiled and said, "We'll get you in there in just a minute." Then he looked back at the two cars in front of me, and started chuckling. "Probably shouldn't have said 'just a minute'. We'll get you in in a matter of minutes. Probably half an hour or so."

I asked him if someone would make sure I don't drive in the pit, and he assured me someone would guide me in. He said someone could even drive it in for me, if I wanted.

I noticed his arms were sort of tucked into his body and asked him if he was cold. He grinned and said yeah. (My car's thermometer said it was 34 degrees out there.) I told him I was sorry and he shrugged it off and said it was alright - it was worse when it was raining. Then he checked my right signal light, left signal light, high beams, and brake lights, and asked me to pop open the hood.

I'm not sure because I didn't check the time, but I think it was less than half an hour when I was guided to drive my car over the pit. I had lots of "good news": tire pressure is good; battery is good; power steering fluid is good; coolant reservoir is good. When Jeremy came back to go over my bill with me, he clicked in my car's information and asked, "Karen?" I started laughing. "Yup. I am a Karen." He started laughing then, too, and told me he doesn't pay attention to any of that internet troll stuff.

I pointed out to him that I had managed to keep my car out of the pit, and he said he was impressed. I noted that it was "touch and go" for a while, but I made it, and he started laughing.

I told him he was great at this - at talking with customers. He thanked me and said that used to be the hardest part of the job for him, but he's gotten better at it. I told him he was beautiful at it, and he smiled and thanked me again. He let me know my words had meant something to him.

When I left the Valvoline place, I went to Haggen's - because I figured as long as it was next door I might as well stop in and see if there's anything I needed. On my way into the store, I saw a little beaded earring lying in a crack in the sidewalk and picked it up. I brought it to one of the Haggen's employees who said she'd take it to the "lost and found" for me. I picked up some romaine lettuce and spinach (and, ahem, cookies and Lindt chocolate) and checked myself out of the store.

As I was driving home, the thought came to me that I should pick up my mail at the Bow post office, and then the thought came that I should see if the Edison Cafe was open. On the way to Edison I turned off on Sunset Road and nabbed some pictures of the swans in the field there. (I'm going to miss them when they're gone in a couple months.)

The cafe had just opened and Austin and Kiersten greeted me at the door. It was so good to see them again - these are the kind of people that know how to laugh with me.

Because I was the only customer in there at first, we had a chance to talk and get caught up with each other. And this is when I learned that Micah, the young barista I'd met last week at Cafe Blue in Bellingham, is a friend of Austin's! They'd met when they were both working as models a few years ago and had stayed friends. Coincidentally, they'd both become owners of restaurants within a year of each other. How cool is that?!

Connections. I love these connections.

May we all find ways to stay connected in the years to come. May we lift each other up and envelop each other in kindness. May we find people to share laughter with. May we find community. May we keep joy and hope alive.

Mother Wind

The wind blows through the tops of the trees
and I feel the Mother-power of the universe
blowing around and through our world.
I send out a prayer for all the mothers
and all the children of mothers
and feel the Mother-power moving through me –
strong and fearless and all-powerful Love.
The wind is cleansing – blowing away the fear
and hate, the anger and greed – they are weightless
nothings in the force of the wind.

The birds sing. The sun shines. The flowers bloom.
The cleansing Mother-wind blows around us
and lovingly wraps the world in Her strong arms.
We are safe. We are loved. We are free.

Made in the USA
Monee, IL
10 February 2025